The Economics of Special Privilege and Rent Seeking

STUDIES IN PUBLIC CHOICE

Editor: Gordon Tullock
  Department of Economics
  University of Arizona
  Tucson, Arizona 85721 USA

Previously published books in this series:

Bowman, *Collective Choice in Education*
Buchanan, *Fiscal Responsibility in Constitutional Democracy*
McKenzie, *The Political Economy of the Educational Process*
Auster and Silver, *The State as a Firm*
Kau and Rubin, *Congressmen, Constituents, and Contributors: The Determinants of Roll Call Voting in the House of Representatives*
Ordeshook and Shepsle, *Political Equilibrium*

The intersection of economics and politics is one of the most important areas of modern social science. "Studies in Public Choice" is devoted to a particularly crucial aspect of this intersection — the use of economic methods and analysis on matters which are traditionally political in nature. Prominent scholars, such as Duncan Black, Kenneth Arrow, Mancus Olson, Vincent Ostrom, William Riker, and James Buchanan, have contributed to the development of the study of public choice. The aim of this series is to promote the growth of knowledge in this important and fascinating field.

The Economics of Special Privilege and Rent Seeking

Gordon Tullock

*Karl Eller Professor of Economics
and Political Science*

University of Arizona

Kluwer Academic Publishers
Boston/Dordrecht/London

Distributors for North America:
Kluwer Academic Publishers
101 Philip Drive
Assinippi Park
Norwell, Massachusetts 02061 USA

Distributors for all other countries:
Kluwer Academic Publishers Group
Distribution Centre
Post OFfice Box 322
3300 AH Dordrecht, THE NETHERLANDS

Library of Congress Cataloging-in-Publication Data

Tullock, Gordon.
  The economics of special privilege and rent seeking /
by Gordon Tulock.
    p.   cm. — (Studies in public choice)
  Includes index.
  ISBN 0-7923-9011-3
  1. Rent (Economic theory) 2. Social choice. I. Title.
II. Series.
HB401.T79 1989
333.5 — dc19   89-2435
                                                        CIP

Copyright © 1989 by Kluwer Academic Publishers

All rights reserved. No part of this publication may be reproduced, stored in a retrieval system or transmitted in any form or by any means, mechanical, photocopying, recording, or otherwise, without the prior written permission of the publisher, Kluwer Academic Publishers, 101 Philip Drive, Asinippi Park, Norwell, Massachusetts 02061.

Printed in the United States of America

CONTENTS

Preface   vii

I Why Is the Rent-Seeking Industry So Small?

1 Introduction   3
2 Rents, Ignorance, and Ideology   11
3 The Cost of Rent Seeking: A Metaphysical Problem   29
4 Efficient Rent Seeking, Diseconomies of Scale, Public Goods, and Morality   41

II Random Thoughts on Rent Seeking

5 Rent Seeking: The Problem of Definition   49
6 Rent Seeking and the Market   59
7 Strategic Behavior, Mixed Strategies, and the Defects of the Nash Equilibrium   67
8 Rent Seeking and Transfers   73
9 Rent Seeking and Tax Reform   79
10 Concluding Thoughts   91

Bibliography   99

Index   103

PREFACE

As the reader of this book probably already knows, I have devoted a great deal of time to the topic which is, rather unfortunately, named *rent seeking*. Rent seeking, the use of resources in actually lowering total product although benefiting some minority, is, unfortunately, a major activity of most governments. As a result of this, I have stumbled on a puzzle. The rent-seeking activity found in major societies is immense, but the industry devoted to producing it is nowhere near as immense. In Washington the rent-seeking industry is a very conspicuous part of the landscape. On the other hand, if you consider how much money is being moved by that industry, then it is comparatively small. The first question that this book seeks to answer is: How do we account for the disparity?

A second problem is that almost all rent seeking is done in what superficially appears to be an extremely inefficient way. I recently got estimates of the net cost to the public of the farm program and its net benefit to the farmers. The first is many times the second. Indeed, it is not at all obvious that in the long run, today's farmers are better off than they would be if the program had never been implemented. Of course, in any given year, cancelling the program would be quite painful.

The first section of this book, then, is devoted to this problem. The reader will discover that I have proposed several solutions, and not necessarily exclusive ones. It could be that all of them are correct. They are difficult, although not theoretically impossible, to test.

With this as a start, I decided in section II of this book to collect a set of miscellaneous essays on various topics connected with rent seeking. These essays are intended to fill holes in the present rent-seeking literature rather than to make basic changes. Thus, section II does not have a single theme as does section I.

I would like to thank many people for their assistance in this book, but most of them are people who made comments on the various papers after I read them at seminars and meetings. Their comments were helpful, but I have no written notes and do not know exactly who made what comment. Under the circumstances, I simply offer a very general thanks to everyone who was so helpful.

In addition, I must thank myself as editor of *Public Choice* for permission to reprint chapter 3 from *Public Choice*. I also thank Michael Walker, the Fraser Institute, and *Contemporary Policy Issues* for permission to reprint the next-to-last chapter. Chapter 3 is in the process of being translated into Japanese for publication in *Public Choice Studies*. Finally, I thank my secretary, Shirley McEwen, for all her diligent work and, in particular, for putting up with what was, until nearly the end, a particularly bad set of transcription machinery.

I WHY IS THE RENT-SEEKING INDUSTRY SO SMALL?

1 INTRODUCTION

During the time I was living in Washington, D.C., I was impressed with the size and general prosperity of the rent-seeking industry in that city. As I grew to know more about it, however, I began to wonder why it was not much bigger. Not far from my apartment, for example, was the headquarters building of the dairy lobby. It was a moderate-sized office building, nowhere near as big as one would think justified by the roughly $500 million a year the dairy farmers were taking out of the taxpayers' pockets. Considering the expenditures that benefit only special interests and the regulations that raise prices for the benefit of similar groups, one would assume total social costs of about $200 billion a year. Given these figures, the rent-seeking industry is surprisingly small.

On a purely personal note, I am on the board of directors of a small company that manufactures, among other things, a moderately dangerous product. We are much too small to maintain any kind of permanent representation in Washington, but when the possibility arose that the Consumer Products Safety Commission might order the product discontinued, we took action. The present discounted value of continuing to produce the product indefinitely was approximately $500,000 and, naturally, we did not want to lose it.

On a contract basis, we hired a part-time lobbyist who put in about two-and-a-half days on the issue. He knew the right civil servants and the type of arguments that would appeal to them. Thus, customers can still purchase this very effective, if mildly dangerous, product. The cost to us (including the chairman of the board and the president both spending a short time in Washington) was less than $10,000. We did very well indeed. In this case, strictly speaking, we were not rent seeking because we were not asking for any particular special privilege or restriction on the market. We simply wanted our product to stay on the market.

In fact, we did have a very modest rent-seeking objective that failed. The container of the product has a fairly elaborate warning about its dangers and careful instructions for use. We thought that if we could get the Consumer Products Safety Commission to either provide its own warning or at least endorse our wording, this might make our life easier in future lawsuits (if there were any). We were not successful in our attempts.[1]

The cost to us in lobbying activity was comparative small compared to the value of the activity. I can give many further examples, but by visiting Washington and thinking about the size of injury inflicted upon our economy by activities there, anyone should be convinced that there is a real problem. Why should investment in influencing government action appear to have such high payoffs?

Think of a steel company that has two possible ways of increasing its profits by $20 million. The first is to build a new steel plant at a cost of $100 million and take advantage of the improved efficiency. The second is to obtain from the government some special privilege, say, a ban on Korean steel, which will produce the same increase in profits. We would assume that the company would make the choice between these two investments solely in terms of the expense; hence, it would not invest in the new plant unless the cost of government influence came close to $100 million. Of course, the marginal rather than the total costs would be brought into equality, but there does not seem to be any obvious reason why that would make a great difference. One would anticipate that the rent-seeking industry would invest about as much as it gains in dealing with the government. Clearly, the magnitude of the economic disruption worked by this industry is much greater than the apparent cost. Again, why?

This question is the main issue addressed by this book. In thinking about the matter, I have discovered a number of possible explanations. All of them have two things in common: (1) with currently available data they cannot be tested (although there is no reason why they could not);

INTRODUCTION

and (2) they are not mutually contradictory. It would be possible for all of them to be true, although I doubt that such is the case.

I have also attempted to explain why it is that the bulk of these regulations and income transfers are inefficient. On the day I wrote the first draft of this page, the daily newspaper had a story[2] on the Central Arizona Project, an immensely expensive irrigation system now under construction. It will subsidize water throughout southern Arizona, and will increase the production of several crops whose price is government supported. In order to keep the prices of these crops up, the Department of Agriculture must take them off the market. The story reported government estimates of $238 million for the cost of disposing of these "surplus" crops whose production was to be heavily subsidized. I do not see any way of arguing that this project is not radically inefficient.[3]

This inefficiency is not difficult to explain if one does not assume that the rent-seeking industry is efficient. But why should it be inefficient? This question, together with why the rent-seeking industry is so small, will be addressed in the following pages. I do not think, however, that I have a final answer. It is my purpose to start research in this area, not to finish it. The reader is urged to make his or her own contributions to the growth of knowledge.

As a preliminary step, let me give six possible explanations, each of which will receive considerably more attention later. First, the public must be deceived in order to get most rent-seeking activity implemented. The deception usually requires the choice of inefficient production methods for whatever the base of the rent will be. Thus, the actual value of the rent to the people seeking it is much less than its apparent value. The rent-seeking industry would be similarly reduced in size. Two articles on this theme have been published, and the discussion below is simply a mildly improved version of them.

Second, the actual cost of rent seeking is primarily borne by the voter directly. A chapter discussing this point was originally published in *Public Choice* under the title: "Costs of Rent Seeking: A Metaphysical Problem."[4] In this case, it is not really clear that there is a cost.

Suppose that the average congressman votes in favor of these various rent-seeking activities almost entirely for the purpose of obtaining office (i.e., winning votes). Furthermore, suppose that the voters do vote for people who do this kind of thing, and that they do not pay too much attention to political information so that large-scale propaganda efforts to change their opinion are wasted. Under these circumstances, the rent-seeking industry would seem much smaller than the rents derived, but it is not obvious whether the voting behavior generates a cost. Certainly, society would be better off if it did not do this, but on the other hand, democracy is supposed to produce a government that obeys the implicit instructions of the voters.

Both of these explanations are plausible; I have no good suggestion as to how either of them can be tested. Furthermore, they do not contradict each other. In other words, it would be possible for both of them to be true, each one reducing the apparent size of the rent-seeking industry to some extent. The remaining four are, I think, less plausible, but I cannot say for certain that they are untrue. They also are hard to test and do not necessarily contradict the first two. In other words, all six could simultaneously be true.

Third is the mathematical problem of *efficient rent seeking*[5] that might leave society with considerably less than one would otherwise expect in the terms of rent-seeking activity. This would be true if rent seeking were subject to pronounced diseconomies of scale. This explanation could also apply if rent-seeking activity had the usual U-shaped cost curve with economies of scale in the lower range and then diseconomies in the upper range, and if the bottom of the U were close to the vertical axis. As far as I know, no one has any idea as to the shape of the production function of the rent-seeking activity.

My fourth and less likely explanation, then, is that the rent-seeking industry is subject to a diseconomy of scale, which is not of the individual rent-seeking enterprises but of the industry as a whole. Frankly, I find this explanation not very plausible, but let me briefly discuss its implications.

Under this model, individual enterprises would enter the rent-seeking industry until the total size of the industry was such that another entrant would lead to negative profits. There should be a race to get in early, and large resources might be used to win this race. If the final outcome is an industry in which the total cost is much less than the returns, then the relationship of the individual enterprise's cost curve to that of the industry would be, to say the least, eccentric. I cannot prove that this is not true, but to repeat, I find it implausible.

The fifth explanation is one that almost instantly occurs to the average economist, and that is that rent seeking generates public goods for these special interest groups; hence, members of the special interest group are likely to free ride. Of course, I do not doubt that this is so, but it does not explain why such large effects are generated by such small amounts of money. This will be discussed in greater detail in the third chapter.

The sixth explanation, which, again, I find implausible, is that people

INTRODUCTION 7

regard rent seeking as immoral and that as a result, a great many people are simply unwilling to engage in it. I can think of no good way of proving or disproving this. Public expressions in this area are mixed and confused, and feelings are difficult to deduce.

The bulk of this section will present possible explanations for the rent-seeking industry's being smaller than one would expect. In papers read at various universities, I have presented these explanations, usually one at a time. In the discussion period, or sometimes as an interruption to the paper itself, a seventh solution was often offered. Since the economists who presented it were first rate, it seems incumbent upon me to explain why I think it is untrue. I must admit that it has a superficial plausibility which explains the fact that so many good economists have suggested it.

This explanation is simply that monopoly rents would be competed away. The congressman "selling" something worth a billion dollars realizes that the other congressmen could do it, too. In the competitive process, his actual return falls to, say, $10,000.

There are two reasons to believe that this "market" does not work in that particular competitive way: one from the supply side and one from the demand side. Let us begin with the supply side. We first note that Congress, like all democratic bodies, is constitutionally required to operate as a cartel. Only a majority of both houses of Congress can pass a law.

Furthermore, it is not possible for different majorities to compete with each other although, of course, individuals can be competitively bid for by entrepreneurs trying to build different coalitions. Granted that all members of any given voting coalition will probably require about the same amount of payment; however, it does not seem likely that this competition would help much.

That this is true with respect to bills, acts, and so on, is obvious. But the people who have suggested this possibility point out that congressmen do individual favors for their constituents. The first thing to say in respect to these favors is that there is only one congressman per constituency so he has a local monopoly. Still, it must be admitted that congressmen frequently do favors for pressure groups who are not entirely in their constituency. There might be competition among congressmen for the business of the pressure groups here.

I doubt that this competition is very significant, however. The individual congressman does not actually have much power, and the bureaucrats with whom he deals know he does not have any power unless he can get other congressmen to go along with him. In essence, he performs a certain number of favors for his backers and feels confident that if it comes to a showdown, the other members will back him on the floor because they are doing the same thing and there is an implicit deal (sometimes explicit) among them. The congressman who undercut would find that the other congressmen who had lost out to his low prices would not join with him in a majority coalition. Once again, the constitutional arrangement, in essence, prevents competitive undercutting.

Occasionally a congressman can get away with calling a bureaucrat who would not know that the congressman was not able to back up his threats. At this level, there could be competition among congressmen to sell to the pressure groups. Granted even moderate competence on the part of the bureaucrats, however, competition cannot be major. Furthermore, it certainly does not explain things like the farm program. The farm program has to be passed by a majority in Congress and can only get through if the farm representatives have made deals with enough other people so it will get through. In other words, there is no cut-throat competition among congressmen to be the client of the farm block.

The second problem is on the side of the demand. Assume that the congressmen can sell their favors, and they compete with each other for that purpose so that their price could be driven down low. Under these circumstances, the number of people bidding for such favors should rapidly increase. If you could buy $1 million for a price of $2,000 because competing congressmen prefer $2,000 to nothing, then the number of people entering the market should be nearly infinite.

The actual size of the industry under these assumptions should be the same as the size it would be if congressmen were able to extract the full value of their services. The only difference would be its organization. There would be a large number of tiny lobbying groups in Washington. Lobbying organizations prepared to lay out the $2,000 would multiply until the return times the probability that it will be derived equals the tiny cost. Obviously, this is not what we see. The total size of the industry would be gigantic in spite of its consisting solely of specialists in small payoffs.

If the congressmen were able to organize a cartel, on the other hand, one would anticipate something like the situation in Mexico in which the politicians obtain large favors from a smaller and less prosperous group of rent seekers. Neither of these phenomena has been observed and indeed that is specifically what I am trying to explain.

As an analogy, consider the New York taxi medallion and let us assume that each medallion is currently worth $100,000. If the distribution of

INTRODUCTION

medallions were moved from its present bureaucratic monopolistic control to a set of competitive organizations, say, private companies, the price would rapidly fall to the actual value of the medallion itself, possibly $50. The number of taxis would also vastly increase and, of course, the prices they charge their customers would fall.[6]

If, for some reason (and I cannot think of a natural explanation for this) these competing units were somehow restricted in the number of units they could sell, then their price would stay up and they would become prosperous. I insert these remarks because it is at least possible that there is a maximum number of favors that Congress can hand out for organizational reasons. Neither of these phenomena would be expected in the case of the medallions, and I see no reason why we should expect them in the case of Congress.

Thus, the theory that congressmen dissipate their own rents by competition among themselves does not fit the world. First, they are prohibited by the Constitution from engaging in cut-throat competition; and second, competition cannot explain why the recipients of these favors impose such large costs on society. Let us now turn to more likely explanations.

Notes

1. We still occasionally do get sued, usually for modest amounts of money, always by people who have not bothered to read the warning. The existence of a prominent skull and crossbones on the bottle is of great help to our defence attorneys.

2. *Tucson Citizen*, Friday, March 11, 1988, p. A–1.

3. Long ago, in *The New Yorker*, I saw a cartoon in which a congressional candidate was addressing a small group of people at a gas station in the desert. He was quoted as saying: "... and when the Smithers plan has converted this desert to a flourishing garden, I will immediately approach the Department of Agriculture...." Truth is as strange as fiction.

4. *Public Choice* Vol. 57, No. 1 (1988), pp. 15–24.

5. This literature, which has now become quite voluminous, started with my "Efficient Rent Seeking," *Toward A Theory of the Rent-Seeking Society*, James M. Buchanan, Robert D. Tollison, and Gordon Tullock (eds.)(Texas A&M Press, College Station, 1980).

6. This assumes the prices would not continue to be regulated by the present rules.

2 RENTS, IGNORANCE, AND IDEOLOGY

This chapter will begin my substantive efforts to explain the small size of the rent-seeking industry. In it I will make some modifications in the theory which are intended to make it fit the world better. The change will not appear gigantic and indeed I do not think it is, but it is a movement toward greater realism. Furthermore, it does not in any way reduce the waste that has normally been blamed on rent seeking. In my "Rents and Rent Seeking,"[1] I greatly expanded this waste, and this chapter leaves that expansion intact. In essence, the quantity of waste is left unchanged, but the form of that waste is altered.

I have already pointed out that the size of the rent-seeking industry seems too small. Let me elaborate the point by a brief discussion of some observational problems with the present day rent-seeking theory. First, the rents do not seem to be large enough. Congressman Biaggi, for example, saved a gigantic dockyard in Brooklyn from bankruptcy by intervention with the federal government. He was tried and convicted of having accepted three vacations in Florida at a total value of $3,000 from the management of the dockyard.[2] This appears to be utterly trivial compared to the amount of money in question.

As another example, the formal lobbyists hired by the Chrysler Corporation for the Chrysler bail-out were paid a total of $390,000.[3] Once again, this amount seems trivial. In both cases it is likely that there are some payments that were not publicized. If they were ten times as much as the payments that are known publicly, however, this would still be insignificant compared to the government action.

Campaign contributions also seem too small. If we assume that the total in the average election is a billion dollars (probably an overestimate),[4] it is still small compared to the economic size of the various restrictions imposed on the economy to the benefit of particular groups. Direct budgetary cost, not counting the increase in prices, of our agricultural program runs between $15 and $30 billion a year. Total campaign contributions from farmers are a small part of that.

Further evidence is indicated by the lifestyle of American politicians. Unlike presidents of Mexico, these Americans do not retire as vastly wealthy men. They are no doubt well off, but their style of life indicates that they are far from being extremely wealthy. Given the total social cost of the distortions which they have imposed on the economy for the benefit of special interest groups, this seems odd.[5]

To take a specific example, the members of the Texas Railroad Commission conferred benefits worth many billions of dollars on the oil industry. They were elected officials, and their lifestyles, both when on the commission and when retired (one served for 33 years), indicate that they mainly lived on their modest salaries. This was, of course, frequently supplemented by elaborate dinners and visits to expensive resorts, but their returns were trivial compared to the effect of their decisions.[6] These casual observations are not the kind of measures that we would like, but they are unlikely to be off by ten orders of magnitude.

If the observed size of the rent-seeking industry seems to contradict existing rent-seeking theory, it is not alone. There is a second observation to supplement it; simply that the rents are normally transferred by extremely inefficient means. Giving someone a monopoly in something is a socially inefficient way of transferring to him whatever profit he makes. Further, in most cases where valuable production controls are provided, they are not awarded to a single person or organization but to a considerable group of producers who find themselves facing a higher price than would be obtained from the unhampered market, but who increase production competitively in order to take advantage of that price. Libecap demonstrates that the Texas Railroad Commission did not even come close to maximizing the profits of the Texas oil producers.[7]

"The CAB [Civil Aeronautics Board] controlled price competition, but allowed airlines to compete for customers by offering non-price frills like free drinks, movies and half empty planes. The airlines competed away, through additional costs, the rents granted them by the prices the CAB set."[8] In the later days of the regulations one of the transcontinental airlines actually had a piano bar on its flights. This was simply an extreme indication of the half-empty nature of the aircraft which was in competition with others for passengers at the CAB price. The airlines were, in fact, not making markedly higher profits than they do today when the seats are closer together, more fully occupied, and less expensive.

Why, then, do we observe both of these phenomena? Note that I have given no extended citations because I presume the reader can simply look around. As a possible answer there is an argument by Becker (partially supported by Peltzman) implying that there is no inefficiency in the system. I do not believe it, but will defer answering it until I have presented a theory of wasteful rent seeking.

In figure 2-1, I show a situation in which rent seekers confront technical difficulties: specifically, that they can only get their rents by choosing an inappropriate technology of production. We defer discussing why they would be forced to choose such an inappropriate technology until the basic theory has been explained.

In figure 2-1 we have the usual demand and supply curves. The supply (CC) in this case is variable cost. The triangle between line CC and the price P_0 is the rent derived by the owners of fixed resources in this industry. We can consider it as wheat land and this is a Ricardian rent. The producers now organize and obtain government restrictions.[9] The specific details of the restriction would be determined by political considerations which are outside the scope of this chapter.

Assume here, however, that the trade restriction carries with it adoption of a less efficient production method shown by the increase of cost to C'C'. The price rises to P_1 and quantity falls to Q_1. The standard rent-seeking rectangle is shown to the left of Q_1 between P_0 and P_1. I have broken the rectangle into two categories in the figure for reasons that will become obvious later.[10]

Let us consider the occurrence of Luddism in early nineteenth century England. Workers, apparently paid by competing manufacturers,[11] broke the knitting frames used to make stockings. If the workers were working, they would have produced something for society. When they simply stop working, society loses that product. Of course, the principal sufferers are the idle workers themselves. When they occupy their time

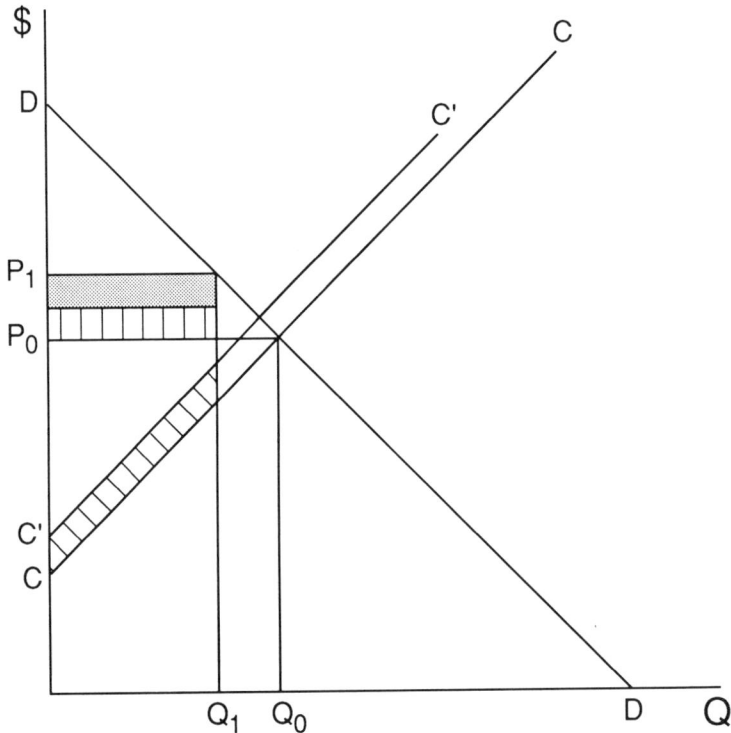

Figure 2-1. Hampered rent-seeking

breaking machines, however, society loses not only their positive product but the machines, too.[12] Society does not have its product but does have a lot of broken knitting frames.

Traditional rent-seeking literature has counted only the equivalent of the broken machines and has ignored the loss of positive product. Thus, the real cost is greater than previous scholars (including Tullock) have realized. The workers not only created illth[13] in the form of machine breaking but they refrained from creating wealth. Both are costs.

We are here assuming that the rent-seeking activity has carried with it not only a restriction but a requirement that inefficient technology be used. Thus, the cost line goes up to C'C', and there is a net loss from the inefficient technology shown by the area with slanting lines. Since the people still remaining in the industry, i.e., those that are not eliminated by the restriction, have to use this technology and it raises their costs, I have transferred this area up to the rent-seeking rectangle where it is shown by the vertically lined sub-rectangle. The actual return on the rent seeking from the standpoint of the people who organized it, then, is the dotted sub-rectangle, much smaller than the total increase in price. This, of course, is a consequence of the need to use an inefficient method.

Returning to our Luddite example, the frames broken were the property of efficient cut-throat competitors. The manufacturers who had hired the Luddites were more conservative in both their technology and their merchandising. Their gain would not be the entire increase in price shown by the whole rectangle but only a portion of it. Part of the increase in price would be eaten up by the necessity of using more expensive manufacturing techniques, shown by the shaded sub-rectangle. Their return on hiring the frame breakers would be only the dotted sub-rectangle. Presumably the amount they spent in hiring Luddites, the rent-seeking cost would not exceed this sub-rectangle.

But even this does not show the total loss. The workers imposed a positive loss on society by breaking the machines. The machine owners' loss when the frames were broken is not directly on our diagram. More importantly, the machine breakers presumably earned only a normal return on their labor when they engaged in this destructive activity. If they had been hired at the same wages to do something constructive, society would have been better off by both their product and the absence of the destruction. The positive product that they could have produced is not on our figure. Thus, the real rent-seeking loss is even greater than the classical literature implies.

While we are examining this construction, let me point out that empirically it immediately explains the low resource investment in rent seeking. The reason that the apparent payoffs to people who arrange the rents are so low in our society is that the actual "profit" to the beneficiaries of the rents is much lower than the traditional measure of the value of rent seeking (in this case, the tradition being only about 20 years). Thus, Congressman Biaggi may, in fact, have obtained the full value of his intervention.

It is not only the airlines and the Brooklyn dockyard where this problem comes up. Consider agriculture. The government program, in general, has taken the form of restricting the amount of real estate that may be used in producing crops. This led farmers to change their production technology so that it used less land and more fertilizer and other resources (at a higher cost because they could have used that technology before).

The current program has been modified to prevent such costs from becoming infinite, but the use of historic levels means that much of the previous technology is retained. Further, the present system prevents certain technological changes that might improve efficiency. More on this later. The long-run gain to the farmers is much less than the subsidy plus the increase in price.

Most government restriction programs will turn out to have this particular characteristic. They are cartels without any binding restriction on the quantity of resources invested. Farmers, for example, for many years faced a restriction on the amount of land they could use, but not on other resources. People can and do invest resources and change their technology as a result of the restrictive arrangement; hence, the profit to the producers is considerably less than the cost to the purchasers. This is in addition to the deadweight loss shown by the Harberger triangle. The situation should be described as "handicapped competition" rather than monopoly or oligopoly.

Thus, for true rent seeking, the total cost is not only the dotted rectangle, or even the dotted rectangle plus the vertically lined area that is the traditional rent-seeking cost. As in the machines breaking example discussed above, there is also the loss of what would have been produced if the same resources had been used productively.[14] Thus, the resources that are used for the purpose of creating rents, i.e., lobbying the government for some restriction, not only are wasted but they are positively detrimental, as in the case of the workers who devoted their energies to destroying machines. The cost is the sum of the positive damage and the simple waste of those resources.

But what about the use of the inefficient technology in this case? The arguments so far appear to apply only to the dotted rectangle, or possibly the dotted rectangle minus the loss of standard Ricardian rents shown by the lower small triangle. Resources used in producing under the technological inefficiency would appear to be simply wasted. We have here what amounts to a metaphysical problem that has to do with the meaning of waste and the meaning of injury. Since we are assuming that government requires this particular wasteful method of technology as a "payoff" for the restriction, the resources involved in producing it are also part of the resources used to reduce production.

The skilled professional lobbyist hired by the farm lobby tells them that if they really want to get a subsidy out of the government, it is essential that they take the subsidy in a form that lowers the technological efficiency of the agricultural sector. They must use less land and more fertilizer. The change in technology is as much an effort to get the reduction in total product and the general lowering of our GNP as was the money directly spent on (or by) the lobbyist.

Returning to our Luddite example, they did not break all knitting frames but only those of the most efficient manufacturers.[15] The additional cost of inefficient manufacturing would also be a cost of the rent seeking. The additional costs imposed by those guidelines which the lobbyist thinks are necessary in order to get the restriction, would also be social costs of the farm program. Clearly the waste here is both the loss of the work the farmer could have accomplished and the additional costs of using these resources in a destructive way.

When we turn to the necessary adoption of an inefficient method of production as part of the rent-earning activity, we have the problem that its total cost may be quite hard to measure. This is because such inefficient technologies may generate external effects on people who are not even in the industry in question. The arrangement under which the airlines flew aircraft half empty across the continent was, among other things, supposed to increase the demand for aircraft, and it quite possibly did.[16]

What we can say is that the industry itself will only fight for a system under which the costs of the inefficient technology for that industry are less than the benefit it obtains from the restriction. Further, it will use resources in the usual rent-seeking method — for example, lobbying — up to the point where the surplus above the cost of production under the inefficient technology and the price that can be derived under the restriction are fully absorbed by the rent-seeking activity.

As the reader will know if he or she has seen my "Efficient Rent-Seeking"[17] and the various articles that have come out of it, I am not sure that this is true. (The reader who is not familiar with this material will find a reprise in chapter 4.) Leaving this problem temporarily aside, the standard approach to the cost of rent seeking, from the time of "The Welfare Costs of Monopolies, Tariffs, and Theft"[18] to the present, has been to assume that there is no reason for the return on investment in lobbying and other rent-seeking activity to be any different from the return on the investment in, say, building a steel mill. If that is so, then the present discounted value of the restriction would always be fully absorbed in equilibrium by the rent-seeking cost.

The manufacturer planning on making money would be indifferent between improving his own steel mill or going to Congress and trying to get a quota on imports of Japanese steel. In spite of the doubts raised in "Efficient Rent Seeking," I am going to use that assumption throughout this chapter. I sincerely hope that the present state of the efficient rent seeking debate in which we are mired in paradox is simply a transitional stage. With luck, someone will solve the problem in the not-too-distant future.

So far in this chapter, I have discussed the costs of rent seeking under the assumption that it normally requires not only that prices be increased but that inefficient technologies be adopted. I have so far offered no explanation as to why the latter should be so, although I have pointed out that it is quite common in the real world. Let us then return to why it is so, and at that point we pick up "ignorance and ideology" from the chapter title.

Consider an efficient transfer scheme. For the purpose of illustration, let us use the Tullock Economic Development Program. This involves placing a dollar of additional tax on each income tax form in the United States and paying the resulting funds to Tullock, whose economy would develop rapidly. Most would agree that politically this measure, regardless of its desirability, has not the slightest chance of going through.

Let us compare the Tullock Economic Development Plan with the Tucson Air Pollution Reduction Program. Tucson is like many cities in that it does have an air pollution problem, not very serious, but still real. While it is an issue that has excited a lot of people, no one wants to engage in the expenditures and suffer the inconvenience that would be necessary to seriously reduce the pollution. This is normal. A number of gestures that have a minor affect on pollution but make people feel good while not being too expensive are all that can be expected.

The Tucson Air Pollution Reduction Program fits. In order to understand it, we must realize that Tucson has a heavily subsidized bus line. Part of the subsidy comes from the federal government, part from the City of Tucson. Since the busses are much underused — I have in all my time here never seen a full bus — the cost of transportation in terms of passenger mile must be extremely high. The busses also in all probability increase total pollution because they run empty much of the time or with a scattering of passengers, generating more pollution than I believe would have been generated by cars carrying the same (small) number of passengers. They are, however, supported by three pressure groups; the drivers of the busses, the small population that actually does use them, and the environmentalists who like noble gestures of this sort.

The Tucson Air Pollution Reduction Program consists of doubling the size of the bus line, and at the same time a research project will be put in hand. It will be naturally allocated to the University of Arizona economics department with arrangements that two friends of mine, one an engineer and the other a locational geographer, share. The grant for Tullock in this program is $30,000. Of course, a research grant is not the same as $30,000 in cash, but not too much different. Each of my friends would get a similar $30,000 and there would be additional funds for hiring research assistants and other staff because we would actually do some research. Basically, the bulk of the money would simply go into buying and subsidizing the operation of more busses.

Given my choice between the Tullock Economic Development Plan and the Tucson Air Pollution Reduction Program, I obviously would favor the first. But given my choice as to which one I should put $10,000 of my own resources into in the form of lobbying effort, I would choose the Tucson Air Pollution Reduction Program. I estimate that I would have about a 50-50 chance of getting my $30,000 as a return on the $10,000 in this program. My chances of getting many millions for putting $10,000 into lobbying the other are so small that the present discounted value is much below the $15,000 of the Tucson development program.

Economically, the Tullock Economic Development Plan, if one ignores the rent-seeking costs, is an efficient transfer. Economically, the Tucson Air Quality Improvement Program — which we will assume has exactly the same cost — is a ghastly mistake. Nevertheless, I would predict more things passed by any democratic legislature like the Tucson Air Quality Improvement Program than like the Tullock Economic Development Plan.

We see the same thing in the farm program. From the beginning and right up to the present, the farm lobby has fought vigorously against any proposal to directly pay farmers cash.[19] We clearly could give farmers as a whole the same benefits they now receive with much less cost to the rest of us by direct cash payments equal to the discounted value of the program, but with no restrictions. This is superficially a little puzzling.

The explanation is simple and straightforward. The farmers realize that such a program would be just too raw. The voters would not buy it. In another paper, I referred to the "public image"[20] as a problem for rent seekers. Citizens do not think of government tasks as just anything. There has to be some cover over any transfers to the well-to-do which the government undertakes. Changing the technology with which something is produced can frequently conceal the real objective as, say, improving total production or helping people without directly paying them. Direct payments would not work.

To take one example, from the organization of the Civil Aeronautics Board (CAB) until almost its end, no trunkline carrier was permitted to enter the industry. Suppose instead of this provision the government had simply enacted a tax on all trunkline airplane tickets and paid the resulting cash to those particular companies that were operating trunklines at the time the CAB legislation was enacted. It is fairly obvious that this procedure, from the standpoint of both the airlines and the air travelers, would have been superior to the system that was in fact adopted. Like the Tullock Economic Development Plan, though, it would have failed passage through Congress. It was necessary to use the inefficient method that was adopted if any aid at all were offered to those risk-prone entrepreneurs who had entered the airline business in the thirties.

Something a bit like this applies also to private monopolies. When we look at the history of such monopolies, and it is a long one, we note that almost never do the monopoly organizers openly avow raising prices and increasing their profits as their motive. They are concerned with stabilizing the price, improving the quality, guaranteeing a reserve of production for possible use in war, and so on. It is true that these slogans have less effect on private monopolies than the similar slogans do on government-sponsored monopolies, but even there, overt choice of purely exploitative methods is rare.

But when we turn to the government and government restrictions, the cover of public interest becomes much thicker and much more expensive both to the rent seekers and to society as a whole. Thus, turning back to figure 2-1, if this were a private monopoly the rent-seeking rectangle to the left would have very little in the way of adoption of inefficient technologies. The lined area would be very small, and the dotted area showing the resources invested in obtaining the monopoly would be very large. When we deal with the government, the reverse situation is likely to be true.

Public misunderstanding of the actual situation is almost a logical necessity for the average rent-seeking activity. Total losses are greater than the total gains; hence, there is a superior strategy available to people who are fully informed. Furthermore, as a normal rule, the number of people who gain is much smaller than the number who lose.

Logrolling is one method of getting through that benefit a minority at a dispersed cost to the majority. It is easier to do this, however, if you are able to deceive the majority so that their opposition is minimized; hence, in a democratic system straightforward transfer from the poor to the wealthy producers of wheat would certainly lose. There are, then, two ways in which such a device can be gotten through. People can be deceived, or the information can simply be kept from their knowledge. Minor revisions benefiting small groups are frequently implemented by the latter strategy.

The average citizen cannot possibly know all of the clauses even in one major bill. Under the circumstances, the prospect of something simply slipping through is always there. The decided risk inherent in this technique is that scandals attract newspaper attention, and the citizenry is likely to become indignant.

At the time I drafted this chapter, Senator Hart had just withdrawn from the Presidential race. In addition, an immense, long series of investigations was going on about the possible diversion of around $10 to $12 million to aid for the Contras in Nicaragua. Both of these defaults, from the standpoint of the normal functioning of the American government, are trivial,[21] but both have attracted attention and are developing into major scandals. In trying to sneak something through, the special interest must always realize that scandal is possible.

More commonly, the program is designed in such a way that there is at least a superficially plausible explanation for it. Designing the program for such superficial plausibility makes it necessary to use inefficient means. Direct cash payments are usually the most efficient way of helping the interest group, but they will not do. The cost of the inefficient method may be high, particularly since, in general, a great deal of complication and indirection is desirable.

Since Anthony Downs' *An Economics Analysis of Democracy*,[22] it has been realized that if the voter does not happen to be pursuing politics as a hobby, he will normally be very badly informed. Indeed, if he is rational in his choice of what subject matter to read in the newspaper, he will be "rationally ignorant."[23]

Recently another problem has been recognized. A voter in voting may be motivated not by actual outcome of the matter up for vote but by a desire to express his own emotions, feeling of virtue, and so on.[24] The voter may, in fact, vote directly against his interest because he realizes that his vote has very little, if any, effect on the actual outcome of the election; hence, he can get a feeling of moral satisfaction out of casting a virtuous vote without significant cost to him. Expressive votes may well lead to more waste than corrupt votes.

Granted an ill-informed voter, who, in any event, is apt to be attempting to express his moral principles in the vote, ideology is of great importance also in the voting. Whether this ideology is devotion to the nineteenth century economic encyclicals of the pope or socialism, it is, in any event, not likely to lead to highly efficient policies. To repeat what we have said before when it comes to rent seeking, we by definition almost are dealing with inefficient policies.

There are two objections to the above line of reasoning. Since the authors are Gary Becker and Samuel Peltzman, they must be given some attention.[25] Becker says: ". . . politically successful groups do attract additional members, e.g. farming became more attractive after being subsidized . . . Subsidized groups try to limit the entry of additional members because that dilutes the gains of established members. One way to limit entry is to lobby for subsidies that are less vulnerable to entry. For example, acreage restrictions encourage fewer new farmers than output subsidies do. . . ."[26]

But either an acreage restriction or an output subsidy would be dominated both in efficiency and in gain to farmers by an acreage payment on existing farms or a capitation payment for existing farmers. In an oral exchange, Becker agreed. Presumably, his future writing will not uphold the above position.[27] He did not offer any explanation for the inefficiency of the present programs as compared to such direct payments.

I can think of no formal test of my hypothesis. I believe, however, that if the reader just considers the matter a little bit and thinks about the way congressmen act, the way the newspapers report political activities, and so on, he will decide that the conventional wisdom at Chicago (mentioned in a footnote before and endorsed in this article) is more likely to be true than the new Chicago point of view as espoused in Becker's article.[28]

In turning to Peltzman, the situation becomes more complicated because Peltzman has never directly said that the outcomes of government activity are efficient ways of benefiting the special interest groups. He does not, strictly speaking, deny that there might be considerable inefficiency. Nevertheless, the general thrust of his argument implies that is not so.

Peltzman says that the outcome of any given political interchange is the result of a balancing of the forces by the politicians so that both sides gain something. Thus, there is a quota put on Japanese cars but the quota is not so high as to prohibit imports completely; hence, people who want to buy Japanese cars are not totally exploited. They would, however, be even less injured by an arrangement under which the producers of the cars get the same net benefit by a tax on imported cars dispersed to the producers. Peltzman does not directly deny this.

Note here that the mere beginning of the political fight usually disadvantages one party or the other. Indeed, Peltzman's argument simply ignores the main point of the rent-seeking literature. He does not discuss the matter, but I imagine he would agree that both the automobile producers and the consumers would be better off with a direct tax on automobiles with the funds derived paid directly to those people who were in the industry at the time that the Japanese cut into their returns.

The movement of the United Auto Workers (UAW) and the automobile manufacturers to put restrictions on the import of Japanese cars immediately injured the American automobile buyers.[29] The eventual outcome of this squabble is decidedly to the disadvantage of the customers, though not as much as the total victory of the producers would be.

In our opinion, there is always, and in all cases, a third participant in the squabble. American manufacturers and unionists in the automobile industry and the potential purchasers of new cars are only part of the people who take an interest. There are also other American voters who are not directly involved. They are apt to vote, if the matter is brought to their attention, in terms of ideology. It is important that the measure be packaged in such a way that it appears to them to be somehow in accord with their ideology.

A quota is a far better way of doing that than a direct tax and subsidy combination would be. These people who are not directly involved in the squabble are overwhelmingly more numerous than the special interests on either side. It is essential, therefore, that a technique be adopted which keeps them from intervening. The inefficient technology is the answer, and once again, that is what we observe. Thus, we do not directly contradict Peltzman; we simply point out that his model is only part of what is going on in these areas.

There is conflict between different groups, and politicians do balance those interests off against each other. There is, however, an overwhelmingly important additional player in the form of the outsiders to that particular squabble who must be deceived into believing that it is something other than simply a fight for pork.[30]

My position, that the inefficient technique is necessary in order to deceive the voters, is fairly easily but somewhat subjectively testable. I mentioned before the existence of various efforts to have minor special interest provisions inserted in bills in the hopes they would not attract attention, and the danger of that technique. An empirical study would suffice of the cases in which the secrecy has failed and the matter brought to public attention.

As a second empirical test, and this case involves a limited number of cases, the dissolution of the CAB and the current sharp restriction on the Interstate Commerce Commission (ICC) both seem to have come at least in part because of the cartel management characteristics of these two organizations becoming well known. Derthick and Quirk's careful study[31] is in agreement.

I would like to end this chapter by pointing out that although I have been arguing that the required use of inefficient techniques is very expensive to society, it may be cheaper than the direct kind of cash payment that we observe in present-day Mexico. If special interest legislation requires the use of highly inefficient production techniques, then the resources put into the rent seeking for it are much lower than they would otherwise be. It is likely, therefore, that the total amount of this kind of restrictive special interest legislation will be sharply lower than it would be if direct payments were permitted.

Consider, for example, a proposal to make a direct cash payment to some group of people, or a proposal to hire them at a price somewhat above their opportunity costs, for building a dam somewhere. Assume that there is $1 million available. In the first case it would be paid directly to them, and in the second case they would make a net profit of $100,000, but they would spend $900,000 on building a dam which we will assume is totally useless. The net social waste in the two cases is the same.

But although the net social waste in these two cases is the same, the amount of rent seeking that we would expect is quite different. In the society in which the direct payment type of benefit to special interests is permitted, the amount of resources invested in influencing Congress would be much larger. In the above case, $1 million is in contrast to $100,000. Clearly more special interest legislation would get through under those circumstances. Thus, the common citizen, in requiring that those government acts that come to his attention fit sort of vaguely into his rather nebulous ideas of what government should do, is probably "doing good."

There is another advantage to this type of inefficiency from the standpoint of an economist. Almost all economists are, whatever they say, actually reformers who would like to improve the world. The particular tools that they have available in this campaign to help the world is the ability to technically analyze various economic projects. The project that gives a special benefit to some interest group by employing an inefficient technique of production is the kind of thing that the economist is in a good position to attack.

It is easy to point out that the farm program could give the farmers the same amount of money at less expense to the customers by direct cash payments. It is also politically devastating to the farm program. Indeed, that is probably the reason the farmers have always been so violently adverse to even talking about it in these terms.

The average voter, as we have said before, is apt to be very badly informed but is interested in scandals. The inefficiency characteristic we have been describing makes it possible for an economist to convert a special interest program into a scandal through use of the tools he has learned in his profession. A direct cash payment does not have this disciplinary connection, although economists — like the political scientists or even the philosophers — could complain about it.

The main objective of this chapter has been to put the rent-seeking literature more in accord with what we observe in everyday governmental activity. We end with the suggestion that what appears to be an extremely inefficient characteristic of democracy may actually improve the total efficiency of the system.

Notes

1. *The Political Economy of Rent-Seeking*, Charles K. Rowley, Robert D. Tollison, and Gordon Tullock (eds.)(Boston: Kluwer Academic Publishers, 1988), pp. 51–62.

2. The congressman has been convicted in another much larger scam. In this case, the amount he allegedly was paid was several million dollars but the cost to the federal government was many times that much.

3. *New Deals, The Chrysler Revival and the American System*, Robert B. Reich and John D. Donahue (New York: Penguin Books, 1986), pp. 204–205.

4. *One Billion Dollars of Influence: The Direct Marketing of Politics*, R. Kenneth Godwin (Chatham House, Chatham, N.J., 1989). Provides a large body of data on the use of money in politics, basically money raised by direct mailing. For individual elections the amounts are way under a billion dollars in spite of the title.

5. For an amusing example of the triviality of these things, see: "Policy Making in Washington: Some Personal Observations" by James C. Miller III, *Southern Economic Journal* (1984), p. 395. Incidentally, Dr. Miller kindly read an earlier draft of this paper and gave strong general approval to its theme. Given his combination of economic expertise and governmental experience, I regard this as a strong endorsement.

6. For a detailed account of the matter, see Gary D. Libecap's "Political Economy of Fuel Oil Cartelization by the Texas Railroad Commission 1933–1972" (August 1977), as yet unpublished.

7. Libecap, unpublished.

8. Dennis Muller, *Public Choice II* (draft of second edition), chapter 15, p. 13. He cites Douglas and Miller, but this is a draft and the citation is incomplete. See also: *The Politics of Deregulation*, Martha Derthick and Paul J. Quirk (Washington, D.C.: Brookings, 1985), pp. 152–153.

9. A private monopoly would be just as conformable for our analysis, and perhaps

in 1890 would have been a better subject. Today, however, most trade restrictions are government sponsored.

10. The standard Harberger triangle and the larger area just below it are not specially shaded. This is to improve the clarity of the diagram. I presume the reader can recognize them on his own.

11. See "Luddism as Cartel Support," Robert D. Tollison and Gary Anderson, *Journal of Institutional and Theoretical Economics*, (December 1986), pp. 727–738.

12. Since in this case they were being paid by rival manufacturers (Tollison and Anderson, 1986), the whole cost fell on the customers through higher prices.

13. "Illth" a word traditionally ascribed to John Stewart Mill, although I do not know of a specific citation, is the opposite of wealth. Unfortunately, a great deal of economic activity generates illth instead of wealth.

14. See my "Rents and Rent-Seeking," *The Political Economy of Rent-Seeking*, Charles K. Rowley, Robert D. Tollison, and Gordon Tullock (eds.)(Boston: Kluwer Academic Publishers, 1988), pp. 51–62, for a more complete explanation.

15. See Tollison and Anderson, 1986.

16. This is a subject of dispute.

17. In *Toward a Theory of the Rent-Seeking Society*, James M. Buchanan, Robert D. Tollison and Gordon Tullock (eds.)(College Station: Texas A&M University Press, 1980), pp. 97–112. This article set off a fairly lengthy series of comments mainly published in *Public Choice*. The whole exchange is contained in *The Political Economy of Rent-Seeking* (1988).

18. *Western Economic Journal*, Vol. 5 (Fall 167), pp. 224–232.

19. Recently, disguises have become harder and harder to devise. As a result, some of the present programs impress most economists as direct payments. Fortunately for farmers, most voters are not economists.

20. Rowley, Tollison, and Tullock (1988).

21. President Roosevelt lived reasonably openly with his mistress (mildly disguised as a secretary) in the White House, and President Kennedy engaged in a very vigorous sex life in the same august building. Congressmen Biaggi, if the decision of his jury is accepted (it is being appealed), diverted more money to Wedtech. Only New York papers seem interested, and even they are only mildly concerned.

22. New York: Harper, 1957.

23. See also *Towards a Mathematics of Politics*, Gordon Tullock (Ann Arbor, MI: University of Michigan Press, 1976), pp. 110–128.

24. This idea was first suggested by Gordon Tullock in "Charity of the Uncharitable," *Western Economic Journal*, Vol. 9 (December 1971), pp. 379–392, but has been greatly elaborated and improved by Geoffrey Brennan and James Buchanan in "Voter Choice: Evaluating Political Alternatives," *American Behavioral Scientists*, Vol. 29 (Nov./Dec. 1984), pp. 185–201. Recent but unpublished empirical work by Gary Anderson and Robert D. Tollison casts a good deal of doubt on the whole concept.

25. See "Public Policies, Pressure Groups, and Dead Weight Costs," Gary S. Becker, *Journal of Public Economics*, Vol. 28 (1985), pp. 329–347. Samuel Peltzman's immensely frequently cited paper is "Toward a More General Theory of Regulation," *Journal of Law and Economics* (August 1976).

26. Becker (1985, p. 342).

27. Probably the basic reason that he uses agriculture for his example is simply that, since the thirties, it has been part of the oral culture at the University of Chicago to say that the agricultural program is inefficient in the sense that direct cash payments would have been better.

28. Becker (1985).

29. It also injured some of the Japanese car manufacturing companies, but it benefitted others so we shall leave that argument aside. In any event, they do not vote in American elections.

30. In some cases, a straightforward fight for pork is regarded by the average citizen as excusable, if not virtuous. The argument that everybody else has a dam in their district and I should have one, too, seems to be regarded as morally unobjectionable. Currently, moral fairness can take the form of everybody getting some of the loot.

31. Derthick and Quirk (1985).

3 THE COST OF RENT SEEKING: A METAPHYSICAL PROBLEM

We know that one of the reasons congressmen vote for such things as protective tariffs and the farm subsidy program is that they think it will attract votes. Economists are almost always opposed to these items because they think they injure the voters. Technically speaking, what happens is that the voters specialize their vote, i.e., concentrate their entire preference function on one particular issue (or a few issues) that has considerable importance to them. Other voters concentrating their voting decision on other special issues ignore the well being of the first voter.

Economists would argue that all of the voters are worse off than if they had not specialized their votes. On the other hand, democracy is supposed to give the voter his choice, not what some economists think that they should choose. The voters vote for such things. Can we count this as a cost?

There is another problem here, which is that voters are apt to be badly informed. Indeed, any *Public Choice* scholar worth his salt, at sometime during his teaching, proves to his students that the rational voter who gives thought to the matter will decide not to be well informed about politics unless he happens to regard politics as a hobby.

As an example of the difficulties here, consider the following from the former chairman of the President's Council of Economic Advisors, Herbert Stein: "The 'problem' of the deficit is to make the decisions as well informed and as responsive to the desires of the public as possible."[1] The problem, of course, is that if the public is systematically poorly informed, then the two criteria are inconsistent. And the public *is* systematically ill informed.

The problem raised by individuals making choices, which from the outside seems to be unwise, is a real one. Do such choices impose a cost on the chooser? Note that in the market and in politics this is a hard question to answer, but fortunately in the market it is rarely, if ever, an important question. If we are trying to measure the cost of rent seeking, it may be very important, indeed, because it may be the principal payoff to a congressman for votes for, say, the farm program is his reelection by voters who are voting because of the farm program. Is this a cost?

Let us digress a little bit and talk about costs in the private market in cases where information is poor. Two hundred years ago, someone who was ill would go to a doctor and ask to be bled. Suppose the doctor is bleeding him with a knife used earlier that day to bleed eight or ten people with assorted diseases. He has never sterilized the knife because he has never heard of germs. Ignoring the germ problem, bleeding is a treatment that will usually make the person worse regardless of the disease. Is there a cost in this? With our present scientific knowledge, the bleeding was clearly an erroneous decision by the purchaser of medical services.

To make the problem more difficult, let us assume it is not 200 years ago, but 130 years ago and that most doctors and patients have realized that bleeding is not a good treatment. Suppose, however, that an old-fashioned patient and an old-fashioned doctor reach a mutually agreeable bargain under which the doctor bleeds the patient, once again using an unsterilized knife. Does this impose a "cost" on the patient?

These questions are not very important for a student of the market, but when we turn to rent seeking, they are significant. Let us take an example where the people are well informed but where there are externalities. Suppose a car driver is polluting the air in the early fifties when there were no regulations on it. He would be aware of the fact that if he stopped polluting the air, it would have almost no effect on him although everyone else in the society — and for that matter, himself — would be trivially better off. Since the cost would fall entirely on him and the benefit to him would be trivial, he would choose not to do so. This would be so even if the benefit from that act, summed over the entire society, were considerably greater than the cost to him. Economists normally say that in this case, he would be imposing a cost on society and would favor social institutions to compel him to either stop imposing his pollution on society or at least pay its full costs.

Let us go to another case which is a closer fit to what we have in mind. Suppose that the society is proposing to restrict air pollutants and that the dry cleaning establishments organized for the purpose of being exempted from the act. They make deals with various other pressure groups agreeing to vote for congressmen who favor restricting the import of Japanese automobiles, favor the farm program, and so on. As a result, they get their exemption built into the act with the result that the level of air pollution is considerably higher than it otherwise would be. Is this a cost?

The last is particularly important because it seems largely true that rent seeking depends on just exactly that kind of maneuvering, and the question of whether it is a cost is important in attempting to measure the cost of rent seeking. Suppose, for example, that we have perfect information and are able to investigate all of the influences that led to, say, the farm program's getting through. We found that misinformation about the farm program on the part of nonfarmers was important. As a result of their ignorance they did not push against it, and the farmers used their influence to get it. These two factors between them are, say, 90 percent of the "causal" factors that led to its going through. There were some campaign contributions, spectacular dinners with feminine companionship, and possibly bribes, but these things added up to less than 10 percent of the causal factors. Would we include the 90 percent in the cost of rent seeking?

Suppose that we have a political system like ones sometimes seen in high school civics texts in which the voters vote in terms of what they think is good for the country. These texts imply, probably not too inaccurately, that what is good for the country is also good for the individual voter. The voter, being systematically uninformed, would make a bad choice of policies to benefit the country. If we turn to a realistic situation in which many people vote specifically to benefit themselves by such things as the farm program, the outcome would certainly be different — though not necessarily inferior — than if they were voting in terms of the "public interest."

As a former Foreign Service officer and a man much interested in foreign policy, I have paid careful attention to the development of American policies in this area. No doubt some of them are motivated by fairly selfish drives on the part of the voters. At one time, for example, the aid program was keeping the American Locomotive Industry alive. On the other hand, there is no doubt that a number of policies do not have any particular selfish group in the United States pushing them.

Our generally vague desire that foreign countries be democracies is an example. In this case, many Americans will maintain, without showing any signs of realizing how absurd it is, that such democratic governments are in the best interest of the United States as well as ethical. Clearly, however, this is a rationalization. Joseph A. Schumpeter, in *Capitalism, Socialism and Democracy*,[2] described American policy as "ethical imperialism," i.e., an effort to impose the American ethical system throughout the world. This is something that most Americans want, although most of them refuse to admit it. Such an objective does not have much selfish benefit for the average American.

The point is that after lengthy study of the situation, I believe that the common good of the United States in foreign affairs is damaged more by the policies that aim (ignorantly) at the general public good, than by the policies that result from rent seeking.

This opinion does not prove that the same relative damage was done by the two different criteria in domestic affairs. What we have here is a case of voters who, if they get involved in attempting to deal with the public good, would do so in a very badly informed way. If the rent seekers are pushing for some special benefit for themselves, they also will not be very well informed and will not engage in much thought about the problem. But the odds are that the policy will serve their selfish interests more than "publicly interested" policy will serve the public good.

It is not obvious that we would object to the voters specializing their interests. Doing so might not cause as much damage as would an attempt to implement the public good.

Another problem is that in some cases we want the special interest to be implemented. My first article in this area[3] dealt with a situation in which road repairing, up to a point, benefited people who lived on the road to be repaired more than the cost imposed on society as a whole. There are many cases of this sort, i.e., situations in which for some reason it is hard for a small group to provide something of interest to them, but where providing it would cost society less than the benefit to the small group. In these circumstances, we would suggest that society provide it on the assumption that all of us will, from time to time, be in the same small group situation.

The problem is that the small group may push for things where the benefit to them is smaller — in many cases immensely smaller — than the injury inflicted on other people. Unfortunately, these rent seekers may get their way.

Our desire to impose our ethical system on other people may also have negative effects. William Jennings Bryan was Secretary of State in the early part of the Wilson administration. His policy toward China, which was an active one, aimed at the objective of not interfering with the rapid conversion of China to Christianity which he believed was taking place at that time. Indeed, he not only refrained from interfering with it, he was in favor of pushing it ahead. This was an ethically driven policy intended to do good; at the least, it did no positive harm.

In a way, the Chinese Revolution was brought on by President William Howard Taft who was making an ill-advised[4] effort to obtain special privileges for American bankers.[5] In doing so, he delayed the construction of some important railroads. The delay, through a set of devious channels, was the initiating cause of the revolution in the same sense that the assassination of Archduke Franz Ferdinand was the initiating cause of World War I.

All of this discussion has been general. Let us try to do a little formal reasoning. For this purpose, assume someone has produced a computer that knows everybody's utility and is able to calculate private and public decisions that will maximize that utility.[6]

Beginning with private purchases, assume that this computer is in charge of somebody's purchases, buying the things that will maximize that person's lifetime utility. In 1776, this computer would not have ordered a bleeding, for example. Compare this with the decision that would have been made by that person himself, assuming that he also had perfect knowledge about that nature of all products and services on the market, but not perfect knowledge about his own utility production function. The last seems a little absurd, but you do buy things you think you will enjoy and then discover that you do not. The computer would not make this kind of error.

Thus, the computer would do better than the purchaser even if the purchaser devoted an infinite amount of time studying before each purchase, with the infinite time somehow having zero cost to him. It would, in fact, do better than any human instrumentality because it would know things that have not yet been discovered. In reality, of course, the individual does not know much about most of the products and services he buys. Further, he essentially depends on other people to make many of the preliminary decisions for him.

I buy clothes from stores that specialize in producing clothing for people who, like myself, are in the upper, but a long way from the top, income brackets. In doing so, I am assuming first that my fellow consumers from this store do at least a reasonably good job in judging price and quality, and second, that the store owners who want to make money by pleasing their customers do a reasonably good job at meeting those standards.

I am to some extent free-riding on the other customers, and each of them is free-riding on me. If turned to such subjects as medicine, electronic devices, and so on, my state of knowledge differs even further from that of our super computer.

Bentham, as mentioned before, dealt with this problem by saying that we should let the individual make decisions, not because those decisions would necessarily be right but because they were more in accord with his utility than any other mechanism we could design. In other words, he denied the existence of my super computer. Since it is only an imaginary construct, I would not disagree with him. Thus, it is probably sensible to let people make decisions of this sort, and, indeed, we can refer to a society in which such decisions control almost everything as being optimal in what is not a nonsensical use of the word "optimal." Those critics of the market system who point out that customers are frequently ill informed are quite right. But once we get out of the market, the information problem is much more severe.

Although it is not widely known, one of the things that the market provides to the private citizens is an opportunity to benefit other people. They may contribute money to the American Cancer Society, George Mason University, or simply give to a beggar on the street. In all these cases, you would say that they are purchasing a feeling of satisfaction gained by benefiting other people, although once again, information can be bad.[7] Indeed, in this case the information is far more likely to be bad than in the straightforward purchase because the individual who is purchasing a feeling of satisfaction from having made the gift will not himself directly benefit or be injured as a result of what the gift actually provides.

Once again, Bentham would say, and I do not disagree, that the individual should make this decision, seeking out whatever advice he thinks is sensible.[8]

So far, we have been comparing the computer with decisions made by individuals in the market environment. We have totally ignored externalities. But now, in talking about government, specifically democratic government, externalities become relevant. After all, externalities are the basic reason that we have governments; hence, it is sensible to leave them aside in discussing the market. The government should deal with them, although anyone who looks at actual governments realizes that they are almost as likely to generate externalities as to eliminate them.

Let us return to our perfect computer and assume that it is dealing with some decision which, due to externalities, must be made collectively. The computer, knowing all and making no calculating mistakes, determines whether some particular government activity should be undertaken and what its scale is. Of course, our perfect computer could also allocate the entire cost of the activity among the taxpayers in such a way that the cost was proportional to the benefit, but we will assume that it does not do that — it uses ordinary taxes. Consequently, there will be probably some people gaining and some people losing. What the computer does is to make certain that the total gain in utility is greater than the total loss. Again, I would like to emphasize that the machine is a piece of science fiction designed for this article.

The actual behavior of the voters is apt to deviate sharply from this ideal pattern of behavior for two reasons: (1) they are not perfectly informed nor are they perfect calculators; (2) individuals will favor things that benefit themselves even if the total cost is greater than the total benefit. Let us discuss these two problems one at a time, beginning with information.

As mentioned before, there is an old and respectable proof in the *Public Choice* literature demonstrating that individuals are normally badly informed in politics, particularly with respect to what we might call public interest types of matters. These individual decisions are apt to deviate from the decisions of our computer in a fairly extreme way simply because of poor information.

This poor information does not, however, mean lack of calculation. Our computer not only makes all perfect computations but knows what other people's utilities are, something the average voter will not know.

When it comes to matters directly affecting the voter, he is apt to be better informed than in matters of general interest. To say that he is apt to be better informed is quite different from saying he is apt to be very well informed. Here, too, public good consideration means that the single person, who is one of a group of 100,000 benefitting from something, will devote not too much time to becoming well informed about it. In fact, if he is well informed it is more likely to be for other reasons. For instance, because he reads farming journals for technical help in running his farm, he gets political information as a byproduct.

When we turn to the individual's knowledge of other people's utility, the situation becomes even worse. First, he may not be interested in whether others are gaining; but second, if he is interested in helping them, and most of us are to some extent, he has very little information as to what will actually help them. In particular, if we look at programs designed to help the poor, it is obvious that the people who design them think that the poor's judgment of what will benefit them is bad. Payments in kind are very common under such circumstances, as are detailed efforts to regulate the lives of the people who are being aided. In a way, the charitably inclined person is like our giant computer attempting to give people what is good for them and not what they, the ill informed, want.

There is an area where possibly bad information benefits society when looked at in large scale. The individual probably has an ill-thought-out set of principles of public behavior and morality which will affect his voting behavior when he hears that something in government has occurred to which he objects. Scandals such as misappropriation of funds is an obvious example, but there is a whole collection of others. In particular, transfers or special regulations that benefit small groups have to be to some extent presented in deceptive ways, which makes them much less efficient than they otherwise would be. This lack of efficiency, however, has the positive benefit that it reduces the profit from these activities; hence, it reduces the amount of energy that rent seekers will put into attempting to get these rents.

On the other hand, the fact that these are ill thought out has a major disadvantage. Anyone who is attempting to sell a significant government reform knows the normal immediate reaction of a simple superficial objection. Because the standard approach of the average voter is moralistic, he will accept moral criticism of the government, and, in fact, will suggest that the government become more moral. But any attempt to convince him that the structure is somehow badly designed is normally resisted, without serious thought or good information.

The second problem is that the individual, unlike our machine, is interested in himself more than in other people. To repeat, he probably has, as most of us do, at least some interest in helping the country, the poor, the people who are suffering from cancer, and so on. But this is usually less intense than his desire to help himself and his family.

If it were not for the externalities problem, and in politics the externality frequently takes the form of a tax on somebody else, we could ignore that matter. We could let individuals all make their decisions in terms of what benefited them and assume that those issues passed by majority vote, be it directly or by logrolling, on the average will be beneficial. They would not be quite as good as our machine's calculation, but they would not be much more inferior.

Unfortunately, of course, governmental activities are externality-laden, and the decision of the textile workers, for example, to push for a tariff on textiles will generate very decided external costs.

Suppose, then, that we observe a set of protective tariffs that were voted through democratically. We sometimes say they are costly because they differ from what would have been passed if the voters had all been simply interested in maximizing the public interest. But are they really costly? This problem is what I have been leading up to in this article.

It seems possible that the principal payment that politicians in the United States receive from rent-seeking groups comes not in the form of elaborate dinners or direct cash payments but in the form of specialized votes. The special) interest group that clearly has a sizeable number of voters who will ignore all other considerations and vote solely in terms of whether their congressman has backed, say, a cotton textile tariff, inflicts an injury on the economy as a whole, but can we say that these votes are in fact costly?

In a democracy, the government is supposed to be controlled by the votes cast. If the voters vote for something that economists think is not desirable, can we call it a cost?

Can we follow the Benthamite assumption that their judgment is better than any other judgment here? Note that, once again, Bentham's judgment did not turn on any argument that they were right but on the argument that individuals knew more about their own utility than anyone else. It should also be pointed out that Bentham would be horrified by a cotton textile tariff.

This whole problem turns on deep metaphysical views as to what the government is supposedly doing. Most economists think of government as an organization for internalizing externalities. It makes it possible for us to reach a higher level of satisfaction than we could without it. From that standpoint, the cotton textile tariff clearly is undesirable. We might argue that the government as a whole is highly desirable even if it does enact tariffs on cotton textiles, but still we can say that the cotton textile tariff is simply wrong.

If, on the other hand, we — (and most economists do) believe that the people should get what they choose, the cotton textile tariff is right and desirable. Add on the prospect that if the voters stop voting in terms of their special interest and began voting in terms of the public interest, their motives for becoming well informed would be extremely weak; hence, their decisions would have almost a random relationship to that public interest. Then the problem becomes even more difficult.

Let me add on a final item of difficulty and then resign the problem to my readers. It concerns the fact that pressure groups often deliberately spread misinformation among voters. Thus, a regulation may be so designed that it benefits some participants in a given industry but not in others, but it would be sold on the theory that it benefits "the industry." To take an example, when the Agricultural Adjustment Administration (AAA) was introduced in the thirties, it benefited the owners of agricultural land and injured hired labor in agriculture. I suspect that most hired laborers would have favored congressmen who voted for this bill because they thought it was good for "agriculture." Certainly they were encouraged to do so by the farm groups' propaganda.

This, however, is within the group; outside you also have this kind of misinformation. The widespread view among the citizenry that protective tariffs are beneficial not just to the protected industry but to everybody, is an example. Suppose that someone votes for something that he thinks will benefit him because he is a member of a special interest group, but it will not. Is this a "cost"? Suppose that a citizen, whose only connection with the cotton textile industry is buying clothes, is convinced that at the very least a congressman voting for a protective tariff on textiles is doing nothing that injures him and perhaps doing something that benefits him. Once again, is this a cost?

The problem here is how much weight we should give to people's ill-considered views about what should be done. The argument for giving them overwhelming weight in private decisions is not only Benthamite but favored by practically all other economists. For public decisions the argument is not nearly as strong.

There is another problem. We have no objection to people making their market decisions in terms of their own selfish well-being. In the case of the government it is not so obvious that we should feel that way. On the other hand, it is not at all obvious that we should not.

I subtitled this article "A Metaphysical Problem." Metaphysics in this case is not meant in strict technical terms but in the sense of a rather confusing problem. Further, it is a problem of great importance, particularly for the analysis of rent seeking. This essay certainly does not solve it. Can the readers do better?

Notes

1. Herbert Stein, "Balancing the Budget) Compared with What? *AEI Economist* (February 1987).
2. New York: Harper and Bros., 1942.

3. "Problems of Majority Voting," *Journal of Political Economy,* Vol. 67 (December 1959), pp. 571–579.

4. The advice came from the Department of State who simply misunderstood economics.

5. The bankers did not want them.

6. We need not worry about the problem of comparing utility between persons; science fiction, after all, is science fiction.

7. See my "Information Without Profit," *Papers on Non-Market Decision Making,* Vol. 1 (Charlottesville, VA: Thomas Jefferson Center for Political Economy, 1966), pp. 141–159.

8. I knew a wealthy man whose foundation provided financial support for tournaments between professional bridge players. I thought this was a total waste of money, but he did not. The Internal Revenue Service ruled that it was a charitable contribution.

4 EFFICIENT RENT SEEKING, DISECONOMIES OF SCALE, PUBLIC GOODS, AND MORALITY

To most economists, the immediate solution to the problem with which this general section deals would be the possibility of either diseconomies of scale or public goods. I have deferred their discussion up to this point because neither one of them would explain the inefficiency of the means normally used to transfer resources. Also, if used by themselves, rather remarkable parameters have to be assumed. Nevertheless, they can be used to supplement the explanations in the previous two chapters.

Before we deal with these two issues, there is another possible explanation that is not so well known among economists. Some time ago, I wrote an article, "Efficient Rent Seeking,"[1] which examined the situation in which there are either economies of scale or diseconomies of scale right from the beginning. In other words, the cost curve is not U-shaped, it is either continuously declining or rising as the scale is expanded. The article set off considerable discussion because it has rather paradoxical conclusions.

We will confine ourselves here to the diseconomies of scale part of the article. As the size of the individual enterprise goes down, percentage return on investment rises. Returns are always positive, so that entry, with individual enterprises getting smaller and smaller, continues. In the limit of this process there are unexhausted profits. In other words, in the equilibrium state of this model, if it can be said to have an equilibrium, the market does not clear. The total amount invested is considerably less than the total gain.

It would seem that this model would explain the phenomena we are currently interested in if we confine ourselves solely to the apparent underinvestment, i.e., the small size of the industry. In order to get the disproportion between expenditures and outcome which we observe in the lobbying market, however, the degree of diseconomy of scale would have to be extreme.

There is a more important problem here. If we face this kind of diseconomy of scale, we would anticipate that the entrants into the business would tend to be small indeed. It would be more sensible to have 250 tiny lobbies pushing for the benefit of the steel industry than 25 small ones, and certainly more than one sizeable one. We do not observe this extreme fragmentation in the existing lobbying industry. If anything, it works the other way, with each particular interest having a single organization in Washington.

This does not prove that we might not have the U-shaped cost curve over scale with a declining portion when the lobby is extremely small and the rising part as the lobby gets bigger. Conceivably all lobbies in Washington are in the diseconomy portion of this U-shaped curve. The efficient size would be at the low point of this curve.

This type of diseconomy of scale, however, does not help us because assuming that there is an optimal size for lobbies and that it is quite small, the total industry could be immense simply by having a large number of small lobbies. In order for diseconomies of scale to explain the apparent difference between the size of the industry and the size of its effect, there has to be some kind of diseconomy of scale for the industry as a whole, i.e., somehow or the other the various lobbies must interfere with each other. Individual lobbies must generate negative externalities for each other.

It is difficult to see how this could be so in the legislative area. Presumably, there is a maximum, apparently a high maximum, on the total number of laws Congress can pass and regulations that our bureaucracy can promulgate. This, however, does not tell us how many lobbies there will be. Suppose, for example, that the total number of laws that can be passed is 100,000 and that each one is worth $1 million to those pushing for it, while the costs of a most efficient sized lobby is only $100,000. This should lead to a million $100,000 lobbies, each of which has a one-in-ten chance of getting a million dollar prize. The total amount invested in lobbying would be the same as the total return. As I said in my first article,[2] lobbying has some resemblance to buying a lottery ticket.

The degree of diseconomy necessary here is both peculiar and strong. It has to be such that above a certain number of lobbies, the net return on the additional lobby is negative. The return on expansion of all existing lobbies would also have to be negative. Even the apparent disproportion in the size of the effect to the lobbying effort, this implies a high rate of generalized diseconomy and negative externality. Although I would not like to say it is impossible, it does not seem reasonable.

Let us now turn to the public goods phenomenon. Ever since Mancur Olson's *The Logic of Collective Action: Public Goods and the Theory of Groups*,[3] we have realized that pressure groups do generate public goods for their particular industry. This naturally raises an organizational problem. The steel mill that refuses to make its contribution to the steel industry's lobby will benefit from a restriction on Korean steel imports just as much as those who do make such a contribution; hence, one would anticipate underinvestment in such lobbying. What we are trying to explain is not that the investment by the special interest is less than what would be optimal, but that the investment seems to be much less than the benefit conferred.

Let me invent an example. Suppose there were an industry with 100 firms of about the same size, and there is some favor from the government, say, a protective tariff that would benefit that industry as a whole. Assume that the height of the tariff is a positive function of the amount invested, i.e., it would be higher as more money is put in by the lobbyists. Further, assume that the optimal tariff, from the standpoint of the industry as a whole, is one involving the investment of $500 or $5 apiece by our 100 companies.

If one company decided to invest $1 and let the others free ride, there would be some tariff protection. It would itself receive only about 1 percent of that tariff protection so that the total value of the lobbying is about 100 times the size of benefit to the investing firm.

So far so good, but note the rather extreme disproportion of our numbers here. One dollar invested by this one company provides almost 20 percent of the public good purchasable for $500. There must be an extraordinarily rapid deterioration in payoff for each additional dollar invested. Indeed, although I do not want to say these number are impossible, they come very close.

This impossibility, of course, is simply due to the size of the numbers. But these numbers do seem to be not too different from what we actually observe in the lobbying industry. The ratio of actual investment in lobbying to the net cost inflicted on the economy is large enough so that the return must be high on the first units invested and low on the units afterwards in order to explain the situation by use of public good arguments.

As a technical aside, there is a possible discontinuity here. It might be that the amount of public goods purchased by the first person, whom we assume has exceptional demand for it, is so great that the remaining members of the industry, even if they worked collectively, would prefer to make no investment in moving to the industry optimum. In other words, although for all 100 of them investing $5 apiece would be better than investing nothing, for 99 of them investing $5 apiece when one of them has invested $1 (and assuming that he has added his $4 in at this point) is worse than free riding on the $1 investment by one. This would, of course, be an extreme situation, but the numbers are extreme.

If, however, the arguments in the preceding two chapters are accepted, or either one of them is accepted, then the diseconomies of scale and public goods might be able to supplement them. The general characteristic of the first of these articles is that the total benefit received by the companies is much smaller than its cost to the economy. For the second, the bulk of the incentive to politicians for enacting certain laws is the desire to get reelected. In other words, the voters actually push things through, not the lobbies. If these arguments are accepted, then possible diseconomies of scale and possible public goods arguments could be added on without much difficulty.

This is also true of my final possible explanation: people might think that rent seeking activity was immoral and not engage in it. Although I do not necessarily see such activity as morally commendable, I see no signs that moral considerations have much effect here. Still, perhaps an ethical aversion to rent seeking on the part of some people reduces its total amount.

Thus, it is not impossible that all the reasons I have canvassed for the rent-seeking industry is being so small are simultaneously true. It is not impossible either that some of them are false, and that there may be some other explanation that I have not thought of.

The problem is a real and important one. Undoubtedly, with modern countries the total cost of the industry's generating special privilege is immense. Further, if we look back at history we realize that before the glorious revolution in England (and. more specifically, before the work of Smith and Ricardo), almost all governments in the world had gigantic special privilege industries, which might be a major reason why progress was so slow. The nineteenth century was a halcyon time in which this problem did not exist, and its partial revival in the twentieth century cannot help but have a retarding effect on the growth of our wealth. It is important that we understand it and the political motives leading to its development.

The particular puzzle, that the size of the effort to produce these impediments to growth seems to be much smaller than its effect, has been the motif of the first part of this book. We shall now turn to other areas that do not directly contribute to this problem, although I hope the reader will find them of interest.

Notes

1. *Toward a Theory of the Rent-Seeking Society*, James Buchanan, Robert Tollison, and Gordon Tullock (eds.)(College Station: Texas A&M University Press, 1980). This article set off a lengthy discussion, mostly in *Public Choice*. The portion of the discussion before 1987 was republished in *The Political Economy of Rent-Seeking*, Charles K. Rowley, Robert D. Tollison, and Gordon Tullock (eds.)(Boston: Kluwer Academic Publishers, 1988).

2. "The Welfare Costs of Monopoly, Tariffs and Theft," *Western Economic Journal*, Vol. 5 (June 1957), pp. 224-232.

3. Cambridge, MA: Harvard University Press, 1965.

II RANDOM THOUGHTS ON RENT SEEKING

5 RENT SEEKING: THE PROBLEM OF DEFINITION

Some time ago, I received a paper for comment arguing that the current patent process generated rent seeking. The author's point was that because the patent being a monopoly, and, in many cases a valuable one, a considerable number of people would engage in attempting to get the patent, and this would be a wasteful duplication of research. In essence, as result of this waste, scientific progress was "too fast."

Most people think it is not possible for scientific progress to be too fast, but most economists would disagree. The realization that too many resources may be invested in something that is in itself desirable, is one of the insights provided by economics. In this case, however, oddly enough there may be underinvestment because of competitive research. Thus, the waste might go either way.

In order to see how the research might be undesirably slow, assume that we have a number of people who have decided that some particular patent would be desirable and have undertaken research to achieve it. Each of them, however, realizes that he is not alone; hence, there is only some probability of getting the patent, instead of certainty. Suppose each of them feels that even if he works as fast as possible, he has only a one-in-three chance of being the first person to achieve the goal.

Under these circumstances, he would plan on investing resources of one-third or less of the patent's true value. However, all three of these people will keep their research secret. Under the circumstances, it is certain that there will be duplication, i.e., literally that the different people who are engaging in it will perform the same experiments, undertake the same tests, and so on, and this, if one looks at it from the eye of God, would be wasteful.

Although the various people engaging in this research will invest resources up to, roughly speaking, the value of the patent, much of this resource investment will be duplicative; therefore, the total amount learned might be considerably less than we would achieve if somehow the whole thing had been allocated to one researcher who had then invested the full value of the patent. Scientific research can progress too slowly as well as too rapidly. In this case, it might end up costing as much as the efficient pattern while producing a great deal less.

What does this have to do with rent seeking? The answer is that my colleague who sent me the paper thought it was an example of rent seeking, and, indeed, it does look somewhat like it.[1] The paper actually took the view that probably something should be done about the matter in the case of patents, but it did not have any positive recommendations. I personally am a proponent of patents,[2] but I must admit that there is a resemblance between the two situations.

A resemblance is not confined to patents. Consider the efforts undertaken by producers to sell their products, whether in the form of advertising or simply providing a pleasant environment in which to buy.[3] These things tend to be, to some extent, self-cancelling in the same way that one person's secret research tends to duplicate another's.

An example of what can be done in this area is the recent change in the billboards along the interstates. They used to be large and conspicuous. As a result of legislation, they are now rather small plaques attached to an information board put up by the highway department. I do not argue that this is an ideal system, but I have no doubt that it is an improvement. Information of the same sort that the billboards produced is now available at a much lower cost, both to the advertiser and to the driver who has an unimpeded view of the scenery.

It is not obvious that there is true waste in the sales effort or the invention cases because it may be that nothing better can be done. In the case of sales effort, I believe something better could be done. I think a heavy tax on advertising would mean that the government could obtain funds and there would be substantially no cost to the advertisers themselves because everyone's advertising would be cut back by about the same amount. The experience with the restrictions on TV advertising of alcoholic beverages and then cigarettes, seems to indicate that the producers of these goods were themselves delighted at what amounted to a cartelization that reduced the total investment in advertising. As far as I know, the people who formerly put up billboards along the highways are satisfied with the present arrangement under which they simply put placards on a large board arranged by the highway department.

It is unlikely that any such tax would go through because the media themselves are immensely influential in our society and would object to this cut in a large part of their income. We do not know whether society as a whole would gain or lose from this partial conversion of the support of the media from the advertisers to the people who are actually consuming. Surely the readers would have to pay somewhat higher prices, but, on the other hand, the government would have a significant source of revenue.

The problem here is one of definition. Should we regard the competitive research, competitive sales effort, and so on, as equivalent to rent seeking?

Assume here that we have obtained divine guidance: we know everything about some particular set of transactions and can make calculations on the basis of this perfect knowledge. Suppose we examine a simple sales case, not an invention, but a sales case, in which a number of people are trying to sell substantially identical brands of soap. Note, I have said substantially identical. Certainly technological progress has been made in the manufacture of soap, which the advertising and sales process no doubt accelerates. One of the benefits from advertising, I would imagine a quite small one, is the acceleration of technical developments in the product.[4]

We can now, with our divine knowledge, make calculations as to the cost: first, the cost of producing the soap; second, the cost of distribution at minimum cost levels; and third, the cost of informing the purchasers of the soap and its possible superiority over other brands. The sale of the soap in "nice" boxes and the provision of the supermarkets where it is purchased should also here be counted as genuine cost.

I think our divine knowledge would indicate that the customers would be just as well off and technological progress would go on just as fast. The total cost would be lower if the various parties producing soap were somehow forced to follow an optimal policy of coordination in their advertisements, and so on. The policy coordination, however, would also require divine knowledge because no one now has any idea what an optimal policy would be.

What we can do is work out a humanly possible plan of coordination and inquire whether it would be cheaper than the present system. Undoubtedly it would be, although such a plan might suffer from the fact that there would be substantially no motive for any human being to actually carry it out. Furthermore, there would be many motives for human beings to use the plan as a subtle, or possibly, not-so-subtle, method of cartelizing the industry.

In a way, then, the people who are advertising, and so on, in the soap industry are trying to create monopolistic competitive gains which do, indeed, resemble in a small way the gains obtained by setting up a formal cartel or getting government regulation. Should we call this rent seeking?

As the reader has probably already deduced, my answer is "no." What I would like, however, is some kind of continuous function in which the costs of competition, and there are costs, were set off against the gains of competition, as opposed to monopolistic activity. For this purpose our divine knowledge, i.e., knowing what would happen if, instead of competition, we had an ideally designed program in which the desires of the consumers were not only known but anticipated by some gigantic super computer, is possibly a useful intellectual construct even though there is no prospect of its being more.

To give an idea of the difficulty, I am dictating this chapter in a room at the Charlottesville Holiday Inn. The bathroom has a note from the management that says: "If you have forgotten or are in the need of essential toiletries (shaving cream, razor, comb, toothbrush, and toothpaste), call our front desk and we will get you a complementary replacement right away."

The reason that the management does this is not necessarily that they think their guests are nice people who should be helped. Basically, they are attempting to engage in a little monopolistic competition with the idea that in the future I am more likely to stop at a Holiday Inn than at another hotel. In this case they have chosen, as hotels tend to choose, a very minor advantage because such minor advantages are hard to advertise nationally. Almost the only way people could find out if Quality Inns also do this is through personal experience or word-of-mouth advertising.

This convenience for their customers is also a competitive technique. Is it true that as a result of having this service (which, of course, the customers pay for), the toughness of the competition between them and other hotels is somewhat eased? Will customers pay more for their hotel accommodations than they would prefer to? I do not know, nor can I think of any way of calculating it. Nevertheless, if we are attempting to determine the costs of competition, this would be part of the problem. I do not even see any way of determining whether the customers would prefer to have this service provided, or have a trifling reduction in their bill.

In competition, it is likely that other hotels will choose to do the same thing. Thus, we might expect sometime in the future that this kind of service is universal for all except the cheapest hotels. Would this be a good or bad thing? I cannot say, but I also do not think that the hotel management themselves have either the appropriate motives or the ability to calculate it. This makes it impossible for them to answer that question much better than I can.

Let us think of the patent case. Suppose, for example, there is some potential new invention that will be worth $1 million if it is made and if a monopoly is granted to its designer. At the moment, the discovery of this invention would require the solution of 12 problems, and we shall assume that an advance cost estimate for solving each of these problems is $100,000. Under the circumstances, it clearly is not desirable for people to engage in research for this particular invention. It might be true that, socially, the invention is desirable because the monopolized invention would be worth less to society than a competitive use of the same product, but we will put that aside temporarily.

With time, however, science progresses, and let us assume that after a while, two of the 12 problems have been solved. At this point, one can imagine someone undertaking research to make the invention. One can imagine, that several different companies would undertake that research and that one of them would achieve the patent. Let us assume that if all the estimates of $100,000 turn out to be true, it is just a question of speed, and Company A spending $1 million achieves the patent which is worth $1 million, while Companies B and C each spend $800,000 and solve eight of the problems but do not achieve the patent. The social loss here seems to be quite severe.

But assume that Companies A, B, and C, instead of taking that particular action, say to themselves: "It is likely that if we start working on that, at least two other people will also start. Their scientists are as good as ours. It is likely that we will not win the race except maybe one time in three, so our laboratories should not begin work on this particular project until there has been further scientific progress." Under these circumstances, all three of them would wait until another set of problems had been solved by someone else. At that point, all three of the laboratories would start working. One of them would beat the other two out and receive something worth $1 million for an investment of $300,000.

The other two would make investments of, say, $300,000 again, but would get to the patent office a little late. Under these circumstances, we have a socially desirable invention, but note that we have it considerably later than we could have had it with perfect planning. Further, the discovery depends on the sort of accidental production elsewhere of knowledge that turns out to be useful.

It certainly looks as though starting off the research as soon as the two outside experiments have been done, having only one company do it, and having that company achieve the invention much earlier, would be a desirable thing from the standpoint of society. Thus, we have here a case in which it superficially appears that competition has led to a bad outcome. Further, we might say that, in this case, rent seeking is the cause of the bad outcome because, after all, the return on the patent is a rent.

Try to imagine what kind of institutional structure would lead to bettering this outcome. It is true that if we assume that there is some government bureau, perfectly informed and motivated to work hard, that with consistent correctness makes up its mind as to when an invention has become feasible and then assigns it to the appropriate company, we could do better than the market assuming that the government bureau had a zero or very little cost. Immediately after World War II, the British aircraft industry attempted to overcome the advantage of the competing American aircraft manufacturers by this exact pattern. One of their products, the Concord, is still flying. In general, the experience was a disaster.

It turned out that government officials were not good at making this kind of guess. There is no reason they should be. They were not subject to the kind of discipline that the private market forces on research organizations. In any event, it is not a good idea to have the initiation of new discoveries monopolized by anyone. Science works best if a number of people, all of whom are independently pushing for things that they think are desirable, are using methods that they choose. Again, the Russian, and to a lesser extent, the French scientific communities stand as examples. The Russians actually spend more than the United States on science, but they make very little progress because of the central planning mechanism. In their case, this means that all the brightest people in their laboratories are attempting to manipulate the central planning system, and only the second level people are actually doing the research.

Nothing I have said is intended to imply that the competitive market, whether it is the market for selling hotel rooms or for making inventions,

RENT SEEKING: THE PROBLEM OF DEFINITION

is waste free. I have even recommended a reform: a tax on advertising. But it is difficult to think of an institution that would work better. We motivate people to seek out entrepreneurial opportunities, invest in them, work hard, and abandon them when the cost benefit projections seem to go negative. Even granted that competition does have the defects we see, it still seems better than its alternatives.

This is also true in the case of competition for the favor of a government. A government does not, in general, just go about the world doing good. It has to be pushed into it. Consider, for example, the gigantic to-do that accompanied the construction of almost every single interstate route. The problem was where the highway would go and where its entries would be. Big private investments were made in attempting to influence those decisions. I presume that the investments were not actually larger than the value of the service. But this was basically a way of seeing to it that the government did a somewhat better job than it would do if it were simply planning in advance. Indeed, the decision by the government to do just about anything is the result of various people engaging in influential efforts.

A government planning bureau, the purpose of which is to plan the government, is difficult to set up. We must try to organize the matter in such a way that the optimal set of incentives, which is not likely to be perfect, are given to optimal people.

This brings me to my definition of *rent seeking*. Instead of attempting to take, say, the total cost of a project, including all of the sales and maneuvering costs, and set that off against the total benefit, I have a more modest proposal. Clearly, that total cost is what we would like to do but cannot. My suggestion is that we use the term "rent seeking" (and I always have) solely for cases in which whatever is proposed has a negative social impact.

Consider a clear-cut case. Suppose that a steel manufacturing company in difficulty (as steel manufacturing companies tend to be at the moment) has a choice between two different operations, both of which will cost the same and, according to experts, have equal prospects of success and have equal effects on its profits. The first proposal is to invest a large amount of money in getting the government to ban the import of Korean steel on the purported grounds that it is environmentally dangerous. The result of this would be the rise in the price of steel, and most people in the United States will be at least slightly worse off than they were before. (I assume that the environmental charge is false.)

The alternative proposal is to introduce some new machinery in its plant which will increase its efficiency enough so that it will make the same amount of additional profits. Indeed, in this case, it may acquire a little bit of semi-monopoly power because its costs would be lower than that of its competitors. Clearly, the net effect on society is that the cost of steel is somewhat lower and most people are somewhat better off. Needless to say, the steel company's competitors are not. I use "rent seeking" for the first and not for the second. This is not, however, to repeat a denial that competition may have costs and that individuals investing in it may be consciously aware of the fact that they are damaging their competitors.

I offer this definition because I can do no better. In general, economists can recognize institutions and institutional changes that are harmful in themselves. We cannot recognize institutions that are beneficial in themselves but which, through the competitive process, cost too much. Again, we frequently recognize wasteful expenditures. The expenditures of the people who are attempting to make the invention and who fail because someone else beats them to it, are wasted in the sense that they have no positive output.

Socially, giving people an incentive to compete in a race may be a good thing even though we know that many will lose. *Subspecies eternitas*, if we somehow could pick out the winner in advance and get him to work just as hard (and, in the case of the invention, start him earlier), no doubt the world would be better off. It is one of the many cases where, if we had knowledge and institutions that we do not have, we would be better off. It would also be convenient if we could fly. We cannot detect that kind of a situation nor can we measure the resources "wasted." Let us, then, confine ourselves to what we can do and engage in rent-seeking research only in cases where the institution to be created is, in and of itself, undesirable.

In that case, it is very clear. The resources are wasted in producing it, and the institution itself imposes cost. If we confine ourselves to that issue, we will be dealing with a problem that we can handle, not engaging in Utopian dreams.

Notes

1. Note that in this entire chapter I am ignoring the mathematical difficulties raised by the series of articles beginning with my "Efficient Rent Seeking."

2. See my "Intellectual Property," in *Direct Protection of Innovation*, William Kingston (ed.)(Dordrecht: Kluwer Academic Publishers, 1987), pp. 171–200; and *The Organization*

of Inquiry (Durham: Duke University Press, 1966; and New York: University Press of America, 1987).

3. Expensive restaurants do indeed provide superior food, but they spend much more money on "ambiance."

4. There are a lot of cases in which the soap is simply changed without any improvement and then the advertisers claim improvement. But, nevertheless, over time there is no doubt that these changes do effect an improvement even if the improvement is not great.

6 RENT SEEKING AND THE MARKET

Rent seeking has, to a considerable extent, developed as a separate subdiscipline, with relatively little direct connection to the regular microeconomics of markets. No criticism is intended here, since its field of study is largely nonmarket activities or market activities normally thought to be undesirable. In general, rent-seeking arguments have reinforced the normative arguments against monopoly and other special privileges which the regular economists deduced earlier and on different grounds. Nevertheless, it is somewhat desirable to link the two fields directly.

Such a linkage is the purpose of this chapter. There should be no surprises here. I will re-deduce from somewhat different premises and lines of reasoning the same conclusions found in every elementary economics book. Possibly the change of perspective may be somewhat enlightening to at least to some economists, but basically my intention is to build a bridge connecting two areas rather than to make any new contribution to our knowledge of either economics or rent seeking.

It happens that rent seeking was originated by people who knew economics and who simply carried over the same attitudes and ideas to the new special subfield. It could have happened the other way. Rent seeking could have been the first part of economics invented; its insights, the basis for developing the rest of economics. Even if this reverse operation is not important, it does seem to represent a minor gap in our reasoning that should be papered over.

My major tool will be the structure developed as a result of my early article "Efficient Rent Seeking,"[1] and in particular, the additions to it in my "Back to the Bog."[2] I will assume that the reader has read that material but not necessarily that he has a precise memory of it.

In review, the series begins by pointing out that we have no obvious reason for believing that rent-seeking activities are subject to economies or diseconomies of scale. Either is quite possible. The possible payoff structures to both alternatives, and indeed with many different levels of economy or diseconomy of scale, were calculated. The general results are paradoxical but under more normal market assumptions, they also lead to very definite conclusions, the same ones that market economists have reached using other chains of reasoning.

Briefly, the basic difference is that most economic activities are subject to a marginal and average cost structure such as that shown in figure 6–1. First, both marginal and average costs fall, with marginal cost falling more rapidly. Then, both costs increase, marginal cost before average cost; the two cross at the low point of the average cost curve.

Although this structure is implied by the geometry itself, it is also apparently true of the real world. Some activities exist where the economies of scale are such that the minimum long run average cost point would be to the right of actual total production, although the truth here is uncertain. As we look at the public utilities, the normal example, we find that they, in fact, are legal monopolies. No reason is evident why they should have sought legal protection from competition if there were this kind of economy of scale. On the other hand, they may have obtained the legal protection because they just wanted to be doubly assured; or they may have obtained it in the past when competition was easy and today it is not. In any event, if there are economies of scale that proceed beyond maximum sales, then most economists agree that we are in trouble. But the bulk of economic work deals with economies that have the U-shaped curve shown in figure 6–1.[3]

My purpose is to demonstrate that rent-seeking reasoning leads to the same conclusions. I begin with a competitive market, then move to one that is monopolized, and finally deal with monopolistic competition. In all cases, I will end up with the same conclusions that have been reached by conventional economists. Furthermore, I cannot really say that I am reinforcing their reasoning; it is strong enough not to need

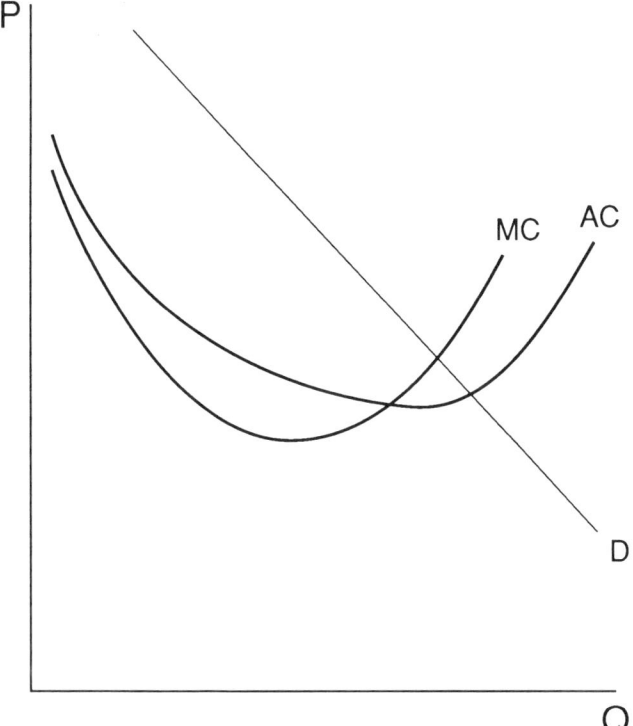

Figure 6-1. Excess demand

reinforcement. What I am doing, to emphasize what I said before, is building a bridge.

Market analysis pointed out that there are strong incentives to bring the situation into an equilibrium where the demand curve, the average cost curve, and the marginal cost curve meet (see figure 6–1). I am going to demonstrate the same thing using a somewhat different line of reasoning.

First, however, we should note that most markets are usually not in the long-run equilibrium described above. The reason is that demand fluctuates and, to some extent, the costs of manufacturing fluctuate also. We have two problems: how the market deals with what we might call short-term fluctuations, and how the market deals with long-term changes that require a flow of resource into or out of the industry in order to reach the equilibrium.

It should be stated that many economists have rather casually said that most companies have organized their production to have a long, flat area at the bottom of the average cost curve so that they can operate at different levels of production with about the same profits. It might be true that the most efficient production facility has such a wide, flat area, but, as far as I know, there is no law of nature that says so. If such a configuration does not exist as a part of the natural order of things, then the company that puts resources into building an efficient plant that had this long, flat area, but that was less efficient at its most optimal point of production than one designed to have the lowest operating cost at some particular point, would be driven out of business in the long run.

The efficient plant with a rather narrowly specified area of efficient production could simply operate at that level and sell its products for whatever it could get. It would always make higher profits or smaller losses than a competitor who had to meet its price. The long, flat area must be somewhat higher at all points than the minimum cost point of the less flexibly designed plant. Thus, the standard diagram from the elementary text that I have reproduced here is fairly accurate.

In figure 6–1, we see a situation in which demand is greater than what can be supplied by the plant operating at minimum cost. This is no surprise to the conventional theorist. He would simply point out that there are now incentives to move resources into the industry because profits are supernormal. In the rent-seeking literature we find a little reinforcement of that position. Using the rent-seeking table 1[4] from "Efficient Rent-Seeking," we see that in the areas of decreasing returns of scale, which is what the rising average cost curve means, there are profits to be made by operating at a lower level of production than your competitors.

Note: profits here are of a somewhat unusual nature. It is always true that running your plant out to the point where the marginal cost curve crosses the demand curve will bring in a larger absolute profit than operating the plant at a somewhat lower level. Percentage return on resources, however, is higher if one holds back a little bit. Conventional analysis assumes that the necessary resources are available to the plant owner and does not consider whether the plant owner might not be wiser to invest some of them elsewhere. Suppose you can borrow money at 6 percent and it would be necessary to borrow $100,000 at 6 percent in order to buy the raw materials necessary to move out to the point of intersection. Assuming the marginal cost curve has been properly drawn, the loan would be a profitable move in the sense that the return on the additional items sold will be more than the 6 percent interest required. For a certain range, however, the percentage return that you are making on all of your resources is less than if you had not borrowed the money.

The conventional reasoning here assumes that the best return on resources overall was in this particular area. Actually, if the company borrowed the $100,000 and used it to get a head start on producing new equipment, i.e., building other plants somewhere, returns on all of its capital would be higher than if the company invested it here.

This line of reasoning is, unfortunately, not entirely general. In the first place, the organization may not be flexible enough to underinvest resources while retaining the same marginal cost curve. Suppose, for example, that the marginal cost curve is drawn on the assumption that the only change necessary in the short run is to hire additional labor because the plant itself cannot be changed instantaneously. The decision to deliberately underinvest in labor, but still try to produce as much as you can, might lead to another and inferior marginal cost curve. I think, however, that this possibility is unlikely.

This line of reasoning implies that the companies who were truthfully profit maximizing will be operating somewhere inside the price and quantity shown in figure 6–1, and will be using their resources which are thus saved to increase capacity. In other words, it implies that they move to the new equilibrium price possibly a little faster than the standard line of reasoning. I said at the beginning that I am simply demonstrating the same thing as the conventional wisdom and not adding anything to it.

Figure 6–2 shows the situation in which the total demand is less than the capacity of the industry; hence, production is on the declining portion of the average cost curve although still on the rising part of the marginal cost curve. Conventional wisdom here would say that resources will now migrate out of the industry, provided that this is not a simple short-term fluctuation. I am now about to demonstrate that this position comes out of the rent-seeking literature, too.

Once again turning to the efficient rent-seeking construction, the company is now in an area where there are positive economies of scale. These economies of scale, however, apply only for the average cost and not for the marginal cost. Thus, the long-run cost will be different from the short-run cost. The marginal costs are such that the economies of scale are negative in this range; hence, the argument given above for being slightly smaller than your competitors would apply here, too. This would not be true if we were far to the left in the area where marginal costs also are falling. More than likely, under ordinary circumstances,

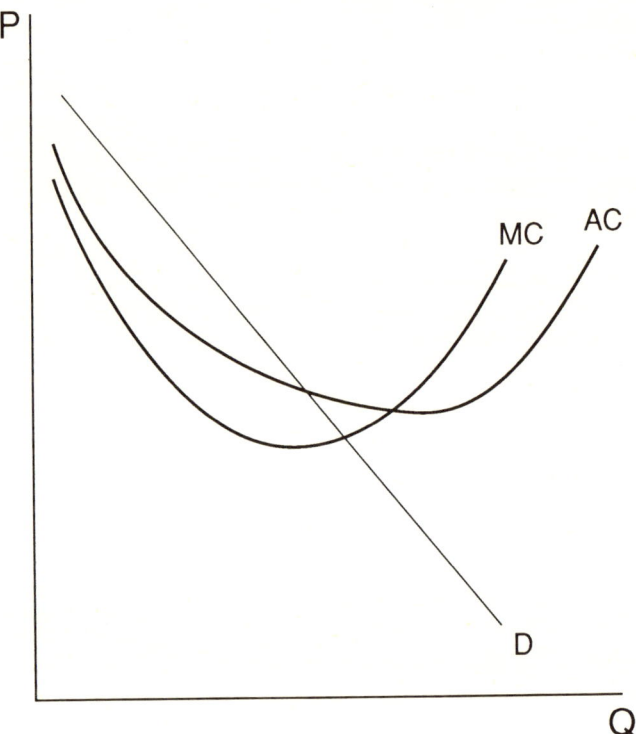

Figure 6-2. Insufficient demand

the economy rarely, if ever, is in such a depressed situation that this would be true, but it is at least theoretically possible.

If the price falls below average costs here, one would again find companies attempting to produce a little bit less than their competitors, but they have a strong incentive to get their resources out of the industry. If not duplicated, the standard argument is at least reached by a somewhat different means.

Let us now turn to monopoly. Here the rent-seeking literature can add to conventional analysis, of which there is little anyhow. If there is only one producer, the obvious decision is to produce at whatever level gives the highest profit. The only mystery comes in cases in which the average cost curve is declining throughout the entire range of practical production, i.e., in the area of economies of scale which are large enough so that only one producer can survive. For the time being, consider the cases in which the marginal cost curve and, for that matter, the cost curve have turned up so that there would be room in the industry for more than one company.

Under these circumstances, all that the rent-seeking literature really says is that the company must invest resources in retaining its monopoly. Such is the general conclusion drawn by many conventional economists. The only advantage of the rent-seeking approach is its greater explicitness. One way it can invest resources is to charge a lower price than the profit-maximizing price. Another is to maintain excess capacity so that if anyone else enters the industry, it can expand and make certain the other company will not be able to make a profit. There are many others cataloged by the industrial organization people. All rent seeking has to say about these is that they do absorb resources, no surprise to the industrial organization specialists.

The rent-seeking work does have one minor contribution here, which is to point out that if the monopoly is obtained through the use of some kind of political procedure, resources are also wasted in obtaining that political support. As far as I know, this consideration does not occur in the conventional industrial organization literature, but it certainly will not surprise the writers in that field.

Let us now turn to the great puzzle of economics: the case in which economies of scale are such that the most efficient production plant is a single plant for the entire industry. According to both conventional wisdom and rent seeking, let us say that in the free market, you will have only one plant, and in both cases there is a certain amount of wringing of hands about what the proper social policy should be. For those who have not read my "Regulating the Regulators,"[5] I should say that my preference is first to repeal all laws protecting the monopoly from competition because I think in many cases these monopolies are not natural but legal. Second, let the companies charge whatever price they want, but tax the full monopoly profit away from them. All taxes have excess burdens, but this one would have less than most. That is my guess. I have to admit that it does not come particularly from rent-seeking knowledge; it is just a general preference.

Turning to an effort to apply rent-seeking knowledge here, all we can say is that the problem is real and difficult. The contribution (and it is a minor one) of the rent-seeking literature is to concentrate attention on the possibility that this is not a natural monopoly but the result of rent-seeking activity in getting a legal monopoly. Again, I do not think this will surprise the conventional industrial organization theorists. As I said at the start of this chapter, I am reinforcing the standard conclusions, and in an area where they are already so strong that little reinforcement is necessary.

Notes

1. *Toward a theory of the Rent-Seeking Society*, James M. Buchanan, Robert D. Tollison, and Gordon Tullock (eds.) (College Station: Texas A&M University Press, 1980), pp. 97–112.

2. This note was a reply to some comments on the original article. The whole exchange will be found in: *The Political Economy of Rent-Seeking*, Charles K. Rowley, Robert D. Tollison, and Gordon Tullock (eds.) (Boston: Kluwer Academic Publishers, 1988), pp. 91–146.

3. It is possible that there are some normal market activities subject to diseconomies of scale from the first unit on. I know of none, but at least in theory there is no reason they could not exist. Artistic production would be the place would should look if we wanted to search out examples.

4. Rowley, Tollison, and Tullock (1988, p. 102).

5. *Government Controls and the Free Market: The U.S. Economy in the 1970s*, Svetozar Pejovich (ed.) (College Station: Texas A&M University Press, 1976), pp. 141–159.

7 STRATEGIC BEHAVIOR, MIXED STRATEGIES, AND THE DEFECTS OF THE NASH EQUILIBRIUM

My objections to the use of the Nash equilibrium can be summed up under two headings: that the simplification necessary for model building in this case eliminates certain essential aspects of the real world; and that, with mixed strategies, the whole Nash equilibrium literature raises logical issues similar to the paradox of the liar.

Let me begin by taking a simple example out of my "Efficient Rent Seeking.[1] Equations 7-1 and 7-2 show the payoff to two players, A and B, in a game with pronounced diseconomies of scale.

In the game described by these two equations, the noncooperative Nash equilibrium is for each party to invest $12.50 and get a 50 percent chance of receiving $100. This means a profit in expectancy terms of $37.50 each. Their net returns will be 300 percent of their investment. This seems an extremely large profit, but the numbers here have been selected simply because they are easy. Similar games with more realistic outcomes will be found in the above-mentioned "Efficient Rent Seeking."[2]

Suppose that A, instead of investing $12.50, invests $12. His expected returns fall by 52 cents, and he has saved only 50 cents so it is clear that in this one game, he has made a mistake. B, of course, gains the 52 cents.

$$\pi A = 100 \left(\frac{A^{.5}}{B^{.5} + B^{.5}} \right) - A \qquad (7.1)$$

$$\pi A = 100 \left(\frac{B^{.5}}{A^{.5} + B^{.5}} \right) - B \qquad (7.2)$$

But consider a somewhat wider perspective. Suppose that A and B have other places they can invest their money. Let us suppose they are engaging in research seeking for patents and they can invest the funds in other projects if they save here. Under these circumstances, the percentage return on the investment is the rational objective. With each putting in $12.50, the net return is 300 percent on the investment. If A cuts his investment to $12, however, the return he receives is 312 percent. B also gains, of course, but his return only goes up to 304 percent.

A has reduced his investment by 1/25, and if he does this for 24 separate research projects each aiming at a patent, he will have the funds for number 25. His percentage return on the total of $300 will be 312 percent, which is better than 300 percent or even the 304 percent that B will get.

More fundamentally, should we be concerned with maximizing the absolute return or the percentage return on capital? If the entrepreneur has infinite funds, or if he can borrow any amount at a fixed interest rate, then the absolute return is the correct number. In the more realistic case in which there are limits both on his assets and the amount he can borrow without facing rising interest rates, the percentage return is the proper maximand.

The difference, of course, can occur only when discussing a portion of his investments. Over his whole portfolio, maximum percentage returns and maximum absolute coincide. But in order to achieve this goal in a realistic setting where the investment opportunities vastly exceed the entrepreneur's funds, he should be more concerned with the percentage return to each investment than with its absolute return.

Further, this phenomenon is general in games of this sort. "Efficient Rent Seeking" presents a considerable number of cases. It is true that at the time I wrote the article, I did not realize that this problem existed.

It set off a long series of comments temporarily ending with my "Back to the Bog"[3] where the special problem of this game is treated in a more general manner.

Problems resembling this are raised by most, although not all, examples of Nash equilibrium. If there is anything extrinsic to the game, and normally in the world there will be, then that extrinsic factor may mean it is not sensible for a given player to play the Nash strategy. Note that what I am talking about here has nothing to do with advance commitment. In the above game it would be sensible to play $12 even after B has played $12.50.

Let me go on to mixed strategies. Hillman and Samet[4] worked out a mixed strategy for a game in which the parties are simply bidding for a prize of $100. The bid, however, is retained rather than returned to the losing bidder. If there are only two parties in the game, the mixed strategy consists of each of them playing all possible values between 0 and 100 with equal weights. Suppose, however, that I (playing Hillman and Samet), play a very high number, say, $95.[5] My prospective returns are the same as they would be had I gone through the mixed strategy procedure and selected a number by some kind of random process. On the other hand, the prospects of Hillman and Samet's losing are high, indeed. They will either have to drop out of the game or abandon their strategy.

The motives for my $95 play could be quite various. I could, for example, just dislike Hillman and Samet. Or I could feel that I am going to damage them enough so that they will be ineffective in the future.

In the early nineteenth century, there were three major trading firms in Hong Kong: Butterfield and Swire, Jardine and Matheson, and an American firm, Dent. They were operating in what could be called an approximate Nash equilibrium. Butterfield and Swire took advantage of a special circumstance to play a strategy roughly equivalent to my $95 one above. Dent never recovered from its losses. The net return to Butterfield and Swire from crippling their competitor was certainly positive.

Another possibility might be that I feel confident that Hillman and Samet are willing to bear risk but not uncertainty; hence, by forcing the game into a situation in which uncertainty instead of risk is the dominant characteristic, I will lead them to drop out and I will make large profits.

Although I have described this in a particular example of a game by Hillman and Samet, it is generally true of any kind of mixed strategy game. If the other party is playing the appropriately calculated mixed strategy, then you may select from your set of mixed strategies one that you like for some extrinsic reason. In matrix 1, for example, the row player might be either risk averse or risk preferring. Note you can do this only if the other party is not doing it and, again, the matter cannot be generalized.[6]

	COLUMN	
	½	½
⅙	+10 / −10	−10 / +10
⅚	−2 / +2	+2 / −2

ROW (labels on left: ⅙, ⅚)

Matrix 1

In this game the row player could safely choose between his two strategies in terms of risk aversion if he felt confident that the column player was a faithful student of Von Neuman and Morgentstern. The column player, on the other hand, might feel a preference for a large chance of a small loss and a small chance of a large gain, rather than the reverse. Either has at least a potential motive for deviating from the properly calculated mixed strategy if he feels that the other will play his "correct" mixed strategy. At the very least, he has no motive for investing time in calculating his own strategy if he feels the other will make the calculations.

John Harsanyi has argued that it would still be better to play the properly calculated mixed strategy as insurance against the possible failure of the other party to do so.[7] Unfortunately, the use of mixed strategy does not reduce the risk in esse, only in posse. If I choose a strategy, my risk before playing is likely to be different than the present discounted value of the mixed strategy. Once I have rolled the dice, however, and have a specific strategy to play, I am in the same situation as if I had chosen one. The mixed strategy involves two stages: computing the random strategy, and then playing a specific one chosen randomly among those in the mixed set. At the first stage I run less risk, but since I must proceed to the second, that is little consolation.

This discussion leads into our final item: any Nash equilibrium strategy may be one that requires considerable calculation to determine, but whose general characteristics are easy to guess. Under these circumstances, there is no need to go through the detailed calculation if you think that the other party will do so. You may be able to make a simple stab at it and do as well as if you had made the careful calculations because his calculations generate a favorable externality for you. In that way, you would save yourself some trouble.

In all of these cases, I have been dealing with situations in which if *you* make the appropriate calculations and play the Nash equilibrium, *I* can do better. The reason I can do better is because of matters outside the mathematically defined game. But these factors are frequently present in the real world. When they are, we are confronted with something close to the paradox of the liar. If you believe in the Nash equilibrium, then it may be sensible for me to do something else. The line of reasoning leading to the Nash equilibrium also points away from it. Indeed, the more correct that line of reasoning, the stronger the argument not to follow it. It is not a true paradox of the liar, but it is close.

Notes

1. *Toward a Theory of the Rent-Seeking Society*, James M. Buchanan, Robert D. Tollison, and Gordon Tullock (eds.)(College Station: Texas A&M University Press, 1980), pp. 97–112.

2. Buchanan, Tollison, and Tullock (1980).

3. The whole series up to 1987 is reprinted in *The Political Economy of Rent-Seeking*, Charles K. Rowley, Robert Tollison, and Gordon Tullock (eds.)(Boston: Kluwer Academic Publishers, 1988), pp. 91–145. The discussion is apparently continuing.

4. A. L. Hillman and D. Samet, "Dissipation of Rents by a Small Number of Contenders," *Public Choice*, Vol. 54, No. 1 (1987), pp. 63–82.

5. See my comment, "Another Part of the Swamp," in the same issue, pp. 83–84; and Hillman and Samat's "Characterizing Equilibrium Rent-Seeking Behavior: A Reply to Tullock," pp. 85–88.

6. See J. C. Harsanyi, "Games With Randomly Distributed Payoffs: A New Rationale for Mixed Strategy Equilibrium Points," *International Journal of Game Theory*, Vol. 2 (1973), pp. 1–23, for a perceptive discussion of the problem. From my standpoint, however, he throws out the baby with the bath water.

7. Harsanyi (1973).

8 RENT SEEKING AND TRANSFERS

In general, authors talking about rent seeking have used transfers more or less interchangeably with monopolistic restrictions. To a large extent, both are the result of rent-seeking activity and normally involve very large inefficiencies. A few hackles might be raised, but it should be pointed out that most government transfers are not from the wealthy to the poor but from the poorly politically organized to the well politically organized.

The Central Arizona Project probably costs at least 50 times its benefits. Further, only a small group of farmers will benefit. It is a typical example of government transfer activity rather than benevolent aid to the poor. Indeed, aid to the poor is not necessarily something that requires political organization at all. Most people are in favor of aid to the poor. Its political source seems to be true charitable activity on the part of upper-income groups. Large transfers to farmers, owners of private planes, and recreational boat owners are far more typical of government income transfers.

But most formal analysis of rent seeking deals with restrictions of a monopolistic nature. Converting the line of reasoning to transfers is fairly easy. Indeed, way back in the past after my first article[1] but before the term "rent seeking" had been introduced, I wrote an article, "The Cost of Transfers,"[2] that dealt with this problem. The purpose of this chapter is to bring that ancient article up to date.

Consider figure 8-1. We have two politically organized groups, A and B, on the two axes. Their expected incomes will be shown by points in the space, with point O as the status quo.

The line SS is the Pareto optimal transfer level. It shows the income distributions available if that sum of money can be costlessly translated from one to the other. Much traditional literature has assumed that this is possible when discussing income transfers.

Assume now that group A, wishing to be wealthier than it is, organizes and invests resources in getting a transfer. This will not be a costless transfer because of the need to invest these resources. Further, assume the rent-seeking costs are the only ones lost here. We assume that the transfer will be made by a head tax on members of group B and paid out at so much a head to all members of group A. This puts us at point R. A is better off and B is worse off as a result of the investment of these resources; society as a whole is worse off. The new Pareto optimal trans-

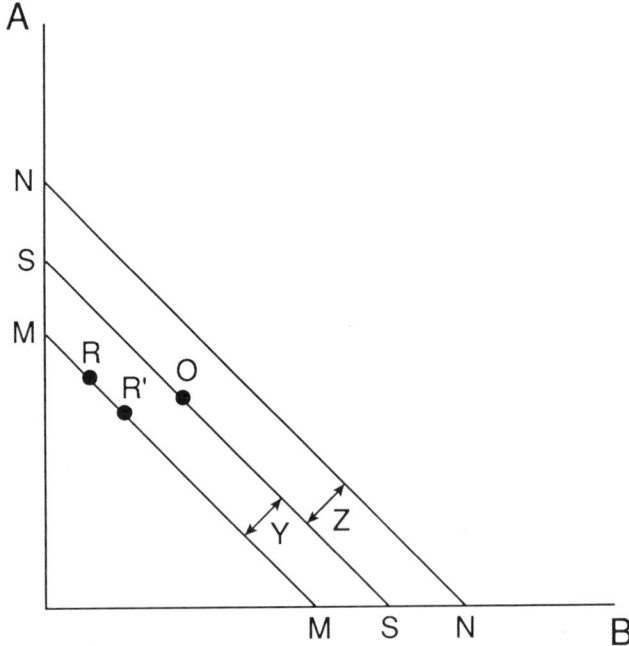

Figure 8-1. Redistribution and its costs

fer line MM is (measured vertically to the two lines) the distance Y below the former line SS.

Note that the total cost of this operation is not really Y because Y is at an angle to the two axes. Y is, in fact, a hypotenuse of a right triangle, the other two sides of which are the amounts that A would gain and B would lose. The cost to B would be great; the gain to A, comparatively small.

But let us assume that group B puts up a fight. While group A is engaging in lobbying to get the transfer, group B is engaging in rent-avoidance lobbying to avoid the transfer. The result of these resources both being invested we will assume is transfer to a point R'. This is less to A's advantage. In fact, in this particular case, it is slightly to A's disadvantage, and although it is a disadvantage to group B, it is not as severe as the first move was.

Note that the reason both R and R' are on the same Pareto optimal line is simply convenience in drafting. There is no a priori reason why they would have to be so. In both cases considerable resources have been spent by society in efforts to transfer funds; in one case, the attempt was quite successful. Society as a whole is clearly worse off even though some groups in it *may* be better off.

Let us suppose that the resources used to fight for a transfer by group A and the resource, if any, used to oppose it by group B had instead been put into some productive use. The result would be a movement of the production possibility frontier out to line NN with a gain measured vertically between the two Pareto optimal lines of N. It is not obvious from the diagram where on this particular line the outcome would fall. It might, like R, be a markedly less egalitarian outcome than O or it might be more. We cannot say without further assumptions.

The total loss to society from the rent-seeking activity is the movement from some position not specified on line N to a position on line M. Some groups may gain. In the real world there are many groups, not just A and B, and multidimensional graphs are necessary in dealing with them. Models of the sort that I used in my "Simple Algebraic Logrolling Model"[3] could be used to show this multi-dimensional model, but I think we can understand it by using simple English.

Let us suppose that vertical to this plane there is another plane showing the distribution of income between B and C. This is shown in figure 8-2. There would then be a set of Pareto optimal planes. With many more parties, they would be hyperplanes. Suppose, however, that after A has made its play in our situation, group C moved. The effect would be a redistribution on this higher set of planes or hyperplanes. Assuming that our simple two-dimensional surface is one of the borders of the hyperplane, we find that the outcome is P. Assume now that D makes its play and the net result is for our two parties' movement to W. Continuing with this process, the cost is obviously immense.

But so far we have been assuming the lowest cost possibility, a straightforward transfer in which resources are used to make a shift in terms of cash taxes and cash payments, and both on a per head basis, so there are no excess burdens. This is not what we see in the real world.

To be more realistic, let us at least assume that the tax used to make the transfer will be a normal tax, one that carries an excess burden; the transfer, instead of being a direct cash payment, will be a subsidy of some sort, so there is also an excess burden. These are additional costs to throw on what we have shown so far. It is not obvious that the lines in our diagram should be moved since they are simply put in for drafting convenience, but it is obvious in the real world that this would be a higher cost.

We have emphasized several times in this book the necessity of camouflaging such transfers. This implies the use of essentially inefficient

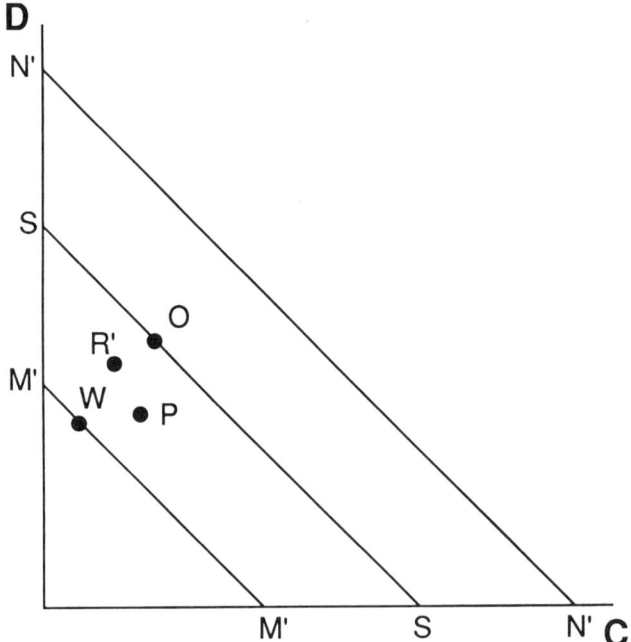

Figure 8-2. Another dimension

methods of transfer because you cannot get direct open transfers through in a democracy. This would be as true here as in the restrictions we have dealt with before. The net result of the use of an inefficient transfer method, say, an irrigation project with the water sold at much below cost, is a smaller transfer and a much larger devotion of resources to, in essence, destructive activity, i.e., producing something inefficiently because only by producing it inefficiently can you get the government to undertake the transfers that benefit you and injure other people.

Again, this kind of activity would lead to less direct rent-seeking costs in the sense of hiring lobbyists in Washington and more indirect rent-seeking costs in the sense of resources invested in something which is less than the optimal way of producing it. Thus, we end up more or less in the same place we were in our previous diagrams where it was assumed that some kind of monopolistic restriction was the way of transferring funds. Frequently, that is the actual situation.

This chapter, which has hopefully clarified circumstances where the transfer is direct, fits into the second part of this book where the point has been to repair various holes and defects in the existing reasoning without making any major revolutionary change.

Notes

1. "The Welfare Costs of Tariffs, Monopolies, and Theft," *Western Economic Journal*, Vol. 5 (June 1967), pp. 224–232.
2. *Kyklos*, Vol. 24 (Dec. 1971), pp. 629–643.
3. *American Economic Review*, Vol. 60 (June 1970), pp. 419–426.

9 RENT SEEKING AND TAX REFORM

As a former expert on China, I know that the rectification of terms is a central preoccupation of Confucian scholars. Therefore, I believe the best way to begin this chapter is with a brief discussion of the meaning of both tax reform and rent seeking. I repeat my earlier definition of rent seeking: the use of resources for the purpose of obtaining rents for people where the rents themselves come from something that has negative social value.

Although this distinction is crude, it is the best I can do. What I would like is a general continuous function in which both the benefit or harm of the actual activity and its costs were included. So far I have not been able to develop one.

The second term that must be "rectified" is tax reform. The common technical meaning of tax reform is rearrangement of the tax code in such a way as to meet some criterion, frequently a rather vague one, of efficiency. There is no necessary implication of an increase or reduction in total revenue.

But that is the technical definition. I think most ordinary citizens are not particularly interested in efficiency. They think of tax reform as having two other characteristics: that taxes go down and, rather paradoxically, that taxes on the very wealthy go up.

A sort of alliance exists between the economic specialists here and the ordinary unwashed citizen: both are opposed to "loopholes." The common citizen thinks that the rich benefit greatly from loopholes and that if these loopholes are closed, possibly his own taxes would go down. The economic expert may also think that the rich have too many loopholes, but basically thinks of the loopholes not as particularly favoring the rich, but as causing a distortion in resource allocation.

This, of course, raises the question of what a loophole is. The most common single definition is a legal provision under which someone does not pay taxes when I think he should. Tax codes are immense bodies of rules with multitudes of taxes and arrangements for nontaxes, i.e., places where the taxes are not collected. Classification of the various provisions permitting the private citizen to keep at least some of his money through loopholes and "nonloopholes" is inherently rather arbitrary.

To take an obvious example, most income taxes are, at least moderately, progressive. No one classifies as a loophole the fact that people in the lower brackets are not required to pay as high a percentage of their income as people in the upper brackets. This is, of course, a clear case in which one category of taxpayers is treated differently than another.

The usual assumption is that there is some kind of a general tax, and that special interest groups have succeeded in getting arrangements under which some particular activity of theirs is exempted from taxation or some particular expenditure of theirs is regarded as a business expense and hence is not part of income. It should be said that loopholes also exist in nonincome-tax-type of revenue measures. The American Supreme Court once found itself determining whether a tomato was a fruit or a vegetable because the tariffs on the two categories of food products were different.[1]

Let us turn to the income tax where most problems arise. First, people listing the loopholes normally treat the deduction of interest on a home mortgage in a rather bizarre way. It is included in the data on the absolute size of the total loopholes in the tax code, and, in fact, makes up more than half of them. On the other hand, when people get around to listing loopholes and their possible elimination, this item is rarely mentioned. As an aside, it is sometimes suggested that the deduction be withdrawn for second or third homes.

I suppose that the political reasons for this treatment are fairly easy to understand, but nevertheless the distinction is clearly arbitrary. In the same vein, many economists feel that an expenditure tax would be better than an income tax because it would encourage investment. I have never heard any such economists refer to this as a loophole for savings.

Nonetheless, I shall introduce a rather artificial definition of loopholes, reflecting a point of view we might call traditional public finance. I am going to call a loophole any provision in a quite general tax that will exempt some particular matter, the reason being that such loopholes do tend to lower economic efficiency. Hard to evade taxes, such as the true income tax, sales tax, value added tax, and, for that matter, the real estate tax, do not much change resource allocation among different uses except insofar as they remove resources from the private sector. They may, of course, reduce work or savings incentives.[2]

The depletion allowance loophole in our income tax, however, did lead to an overinvestment in oil exploration. Most of the other special provisions have similar characteristics.

Note, loopholes that switch resources may have a constructive purpose. For military reasons, for example, it may be desirable that we have some particular industry that could not support itself without a subsidy. To take another widespread example, the American tax code provides exemptions for money contributed to one of a large variety of tax-exempt charitable organizations. Apparently the American people feel that these institutions should be subsidized but mistrust Congress' ability to decide which particular charity should receive which particular subsidy. This system permits the subsidy to be allocated by individual citizens rather than by Congress. I would not argue that it is an ideally efficient system, but, clearly, it is possible to argue that it is desirable.

Leaving these cases aside, the bulk of such special provisions are the result of lobbying by special interest groups. Indeed, that is probably also true of the charitable exemptions, at least in the United States. Most of the special interest groups would argue that production of milk, gloves, or whatever should be subsidized by the government; hence, the exemption is desirable. I was particularly intrigued by the lengthy treatment of the breeding of race horses in our former income tax law.

Suppose then, that a well-organized lobby appears and proposes to get the taxes lowered on some special industry. To go back to our earlier definition of rent seeking, whether this is rent seeking will depend on both the tax and the expenditure side.

The first question is whether the reduction of this particular tax will lead to a shift of resources with the result that the economy as a whole is worse off. Suppose, in order to keep this particular case pure, that the result of the loophole will be not only that some one particular industry, say, glove manufacturing, is exempted from tax, but that the rest of the tax structure will be raised so that all other industries have a slightly higher tax. Clearly, this would make society worse off.

But let us suppose that instead of raising other taxes when this loophole is generated, government expenditures are cut back. Then the question of whether this is desirable depends on where the money saving is made. It is true that there will still be some distortion in the manufacturing industry, but it could easily be a minor factor compared to the impact of the expenditure cut. Suppose, for example, that the necessary saving is made by abolishing the British Columbia Egg Board.[3] It is unlikely that the distortion of the economy caused by exempting the glove industry from taxation would be as great as the distortion that would be relieved by the abolition of the Egg Board.

To take an example equally extreme on the other side, let us suppose that the reduction in expenditures cut the Environmental Protection Administration in such a way that the amount of air pollution rises considerably. In this case, the damage of the loophole could be extensive. There is, first, the distortion of the manufacturing industry and, second, increased air pollution. We would clearly classify this act as rent seeking.

Note that from the standpoint of the people organizing the lobby, this distinction is irrelevant. They are trying to make money by manipulating the government. They do not care about the secondary consequences, and yet we are classifying their activity as rent seeking or nonrent seeking solely in terms of those secondary consequences.

Lobbyists sometimes lobby for things that are of general benefit. I read an article in the *Washington Post*[4] some years ago about what they called the "Christmas tree" committee of Congress. To the indignation of the *Post*, the committee with jurisdiction over tariffs was listening to various industry representatives and then doing what they asked. But the intellectual climate of opinion had changed since the twenties, and these industries were asking for reductions in tariffs. In general, they wanted an elimination of the tariff on their raw materials or components.

The *Washington Post* was correct in identifying this instance as perfectly ordinary lobbying activity by special interest groups. The lobbyists were of the standard industrial variety. Nevertheless, there is no doubt that the net effect of these tax cuts, if less desirable than simply abolishing the protective tariff as a whole, was nevertheless desirable. Loopholes in a bad tax code may be better than no loopholes in a bad tax code. This is particularly so because, in this case, there was practically no

RENT SEEKING AND TAX REFORM

revenue effect. Most of the tariffs under their scrutiny had been set high enough so that nothing was being imported under them anyway.

Long ago, when I first wrote "Problems of Majority Voting"[5] the tiny acorn from which *The Calculus of Consent*[6] sprang, I pointed out that not only are special interest expenditures funded by general taxation but special interest loopholes could be funded by reducing general interest expenditures. The model that I presented then can be best seen by considering figure 9-1.

There is a continuous tendency for revenues from general taxation to be used for special interest expenditures and to relieve special interest groups of their taxes, i.e., fund loopholes. Similarly, the general interest type of government expenditure is continuously attrited by transferring funds to expenditures that benefit special interests and to tax loopholes that reduce the total amount of money available.

Not all special interest tax exemptions (again, I refer to the charitable exemption) are undesirable on general grounds, nor do all special interest expenditures cost more than they are worth. But it is probably true that substantially all special expenditures for limited groups of people and tax loopholes that affect special interests are the result of lobbying. In some cases, however, this lobbying conveys a positive benefit

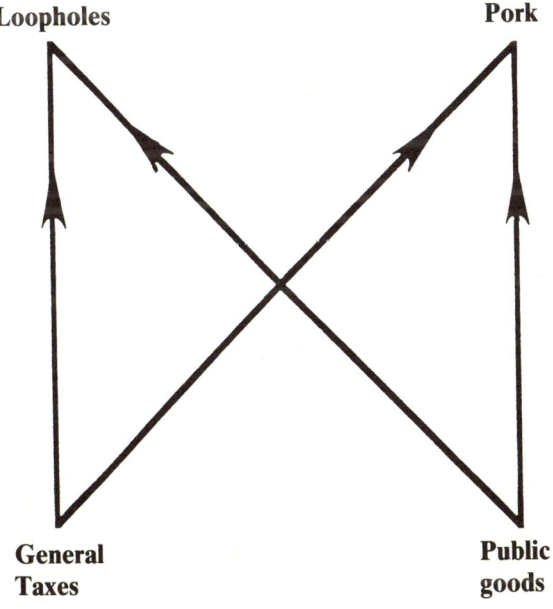

Figure 9-1. The path of pressure

to the citizenry, and, in some cases, in any event, it does no harm. In only a portion of these cases can we refer to rent seeking, following my crude distinction between rent seeking and nonrent seeking activities.

Like most economists, I would like to see government shift to a general tax system with no loopholes except, possibly, for industries where a special subsidy genuinely is desirable. Even there I would prefer that the subsidy be a direct rather than an indirect one. I would also like to have the government discontinue the wide range of activities that actually lowers the efficiency of the economy. The present tax loopholes would be abolished, as well as a large number of government expenditures, resulting in a much lower but quite general tax level.

Clearly, most representatives of special interest would be delighted with this reform, with the sole provision that it does not touch their particular special interest, only all the others. The special interest groups that object to this kind of reform, and they are quite numerous, are generally engaging in straightforward rent seeking. Unfortunately, they are also engaging in what is likely to be quite a politically successful activity.

Public Choice scholars for a long time have pointed out that it is very hard to get rid of individual loopholes or individual pork barrel government expenditures, but since on the whole they injure everyone, a general agreement to abolish all of them would be not only in the public interest but also likely to pass. The problems are two. First, the public is not very well informed on this issue, or for that matter on anything else, and the need to engage in a single all-or-none reduction rather than a series of small steps makes it difficult to pass through political channels. Second, the special interest groups are all very well informed and will fight to the death for their own particular cause.

If the automobile industry could get all tariffs and quotas on everything except automobiles repealed, it would be greatly to their interest. They would even be better off if all tariffs were repealed, together with all pork barrel legislation. But here we have the characteristic prisoner's dilemma. The industry's best possible strategy is to get everything else repealed and retain its special privilege. If everybody tries that, we are likely to end up in the lower right) hand instead of the upper left-hand corner of the multi-dimensional prisoner's dilemma matrix.

It was encouraging that President Reagan was able to get through a quite general change in our tax code in the direction that I have been discussing. Of course, the bill as enacted was a long way from perfect, and various special interests were indeed protected. Perhaps one of the reasons the bill went through was that we are currently depending heavily on deficit financing; hence, lobbies who favor particular expenditures were not worried about taxes to support those expenditures.

It is probably not entirely a coincidence that Senator Mondale in his Presidential campaign came out in favor of increasing taxes, and Governor Dukakis refused to foreswear such an increase. Although this point of view was un-Democratic, its intention was to rally all of the pork barrel lobbies on their side.

We are beginning to get into a situation in which those people who want to cut taxes, either the economists who want general reductions or the special interest groups who want loopholes, are being thrown into a fairly direct conflict with those who want expenditures increased or, at least, held constant. Again, on the expenditure increase side there are the pork barrel expenditures and the more general expenditures.

The tendency that I described earlier, for things to go from the general to the particular, would seem to indicate that expenditures on such matters as improving our military machine are apt to be dropped in favor of special interest groups. It should be emphasized that a very important special interest group is the officer corps and the civil servants of the Department of the Defense. We have one officer for every seven enlisted men (mainly field grade and up), and one admiral on service in Washington for every single deep draft vessel we own. Firing three-quarters of all field grade and flag officers would surely improve our military establishment while at the same time saving money. Unfortunately, this is the case where very well organized special interest groups will not only fight but no doubt win.

Aid to the poor is one area where an interest group exists but does not seem very effective. Clearly, the poor are supportive, using any political assets available to get such aid. In practice, however, results are poor. As one example, people in the second decile from the bottom receive larger transfers than those in the bottom decile.[7] As another, in the middle of the nineteenth century the poor, relatively speaking, were doing as well as they are now.[8]

The apparent explanation is that the poor are poor because they are not terribly competent people. In some cases, their lack of competence comes from perfectly genuine organic illnesses. This lack of competence apparently carries over into the political sphere. As special interest groups, they are relatively inept, and the money they do receive, I think, largely reflects charitable impulses of the upper income groups. In any event, it is not clear that the poor engage in any significant amount of lobbying. There are, of course, various middle class civil servants and social workers who lobby in the name of the poor, although not very much money actually gets to the poor.

Perhaps it is best to deviate here and discuss what we might call the economist's ideal of taxation. First, in a new country, confiscatory taxation of land site values has much to commend it. What one wants, of course, is to have the land value confiscated by the state because there is no excess burden there, while retaining for the land speculator full return on his investment of talent. It is difficult to do in areas already settled, but in areas not yet occupied, selling land at auction with some kind of agreement as to what kind of land taxes will be collected in the future more or less suits these conditions.

The second area that most economists would favor is the taxation of things which, if left to themselves, will be over produced. Air pollution is an obvious example. In this case, provided the tax is properly calculated, there is no excess burden and actually an excess benefit.

Unfortunately, in both of these cases resources may be invested to create inefficient institutions. For example, people may wish to receive the land free, possibly because from their personal standpoint its highest value is as an occasional resource for camping trips. Similarly, people may invest resources in arranging that the pollution tax be either too high or too low.[9]

These costless, or nearly costless, taxes are not large enough to support most modern governments. This leaves us with two other kinds of taxes. One is general taxes, the classical place for loopholes to occur, and also what economists refer to when they talk about tax reform.

Before turning to that area, however, let me mention one other important area. The government has many activities, the impact of which is quite widespread but not spread over the entire population. In such cases the obvious solution is a user tax, but it may be difficult to arrange such a tax. The weather bureau, for example, is of far more importance for farmers and people proposing to fly than it is for office workers. It is hard to see, however, how we could tax the beneficiary groups without taxing others.

In this area, we should look first at the possibility of taxing the users. In the United States, the road system is paid for partly out of gasoline taxes and partly out of real estate taxes by local governments. As a rough rule of thumb, the major highways are paid for by the gas taxes and the local feeder roads by real estate taxes. There is no reason to believe that

RENT SEEKING AND TAX REFORM

this arrangement even closely approximates an ideal allocation, but, nevertheless, it is far from pathological.

For those services for which this kind of funding is difficult, however, economically there is something to be said for relying on general taxes. After all, over our lifetimes most of us will benefit about as much from these things as we will be injured by the taxes if we take the whole bundle of such services.

But that is an economic judgment, not a political one. If special services for special groups are funded out of general taxation, then rent seeking by those special groups is likely to lead to overexpenditure. Many years ago, James Buchanan suggested a solution: we could select some other group of people, perhaps at random, of about the same size as the benefited group and put the tax on them. Thus, we would have two lobbying groups fighting each other and the outcome, presumably, would be improved.[10]

One way of doing this is to change our present budget procedures to a more traditional system. If we go back in history, we usually find that there is no such thing as a government budget. Individual government services are paid for by allocating specific taxes or parts of specific taxes to them. The Lord High Admiral of Spain, for example, collected one gold guinea from every ship which called at a Spanish port. The only way of raising his revenue was either to encourage more shipping to call into Spanish ports, or possibly to fight it out with the other government bureaus for a share of their taxes.

We can easily imagine this situation under present circumstances. Taxes could be allocated to individual bureaus, with the very large tax sources being broken up. The Department of Defense, to take an example at random, might receive 75 percent of the personal income taxes, or possibly all of the income taxes collected from people whose income is in the top fifth of the distribution pyramid.

This would mean that individual bureaucracies and the rent seeking groups would, in essence, be put in a position where their success would depend on dealing with somewhat similar sized opposing groups. I think it would lead to more efficient allocation of resources than our present method, although I certainly would not be willing to argue that it would optimize in any theoretical sense. The objective would be to set lobbyists and special interest groups against each other. It should be noted that whether the lobbyists were rent seekers would depend more or less on which side they were on and might vary from budget year to budget year.

Suppose, for example, in the middle of a major war the upper-income taxpayers, who are by our system paying the entire cost of the armed forces, were lobbying for reduced expenditure, and the military suppliers, including the officer corps, were lobbying for an increase. We might argue that the upper income people are the rent seekers in this case. As soon as the war is over, it becomes desirable to sharply cut back the size of the army (assuming we won), and we would begin listing the defense suppliers and the officer corps as rent seekers and stop calling the wealthy taxpayers rent seekers. This is the result of the crude distinction I gave before, and may I repeat my wish that somebody would improve on it.

All of this has been a digression on optimal taxation. It is unlikely we will have optimal taxation, of course, and what we actually see when we contemplate tax legislation usually is a major effort to make the tax system less efficient and to spend what money is derived in wasteful ways. Obviously, this is clear-cut rent seeking.

If we aim to put a special tax on the beneficiaries of some service for which the externality is genuine but not covering the entire population, we expect defensive rent seeking. We expect rent-seeking activity to open holes for special groups in general taxes and to divert the revenues of special and general taxes to special expenditures. It is only when the rent seekers seek a loophole and the revenue lost by that loophole will be compensated by the discontinuance of a wasteful expenditure that we can regard the activity of the lobbyists as not rent seeking. Mainly, rent seeking in the tax reform area is as undesirable as in other areas.

Indeed, when lobbyists engage in an effort to create loopholes, whether it is rent seeking depends on the criterion of how the money would have been spent had they not created the loophole. We favor special interest groups who seek to reduce government expenditures by saving themselves from taxation, if the reduction in government expenditures itself is desirable. When that is not so, we can call it rent seeking and condemn it. To reiterate a theme underlying the bulk of this book, this concept of rent seeking is a crude one. At the moment, however, it is the best we can do.

In summary, then, tax reform is difficult. If successful, however, it can be used to greatly reduce rent seeking and other kinds of government waste. Unfortunately, the rent seekers have motives to prevent this kind of a "reform." Fortunately, their opposition is not necessarily decisive. A general bargain in which everyone loses their special privileges is apt to be beneficial for everyone. With sufficient political ingenuity and work, sometimes this situation is possible.

Notes

1. A distant relative of mine who was a scientist specializing in brewing techniques once spent a great deal of time and energy developing something that tasted like wine but technically was beer. The advantage was, of course, in the tax.

2. If the money is spent on genuine public goods, the result of the whole package may be to increase such incentives.

3. The Egg Board is self-supporting, but the amounts that it now charges the egg producers could be retained for some other purpose while the board itself is terminated.

4. This citation is now lost. For anyone who wants to try to find it, I do remember that it was on the first page.

5. *Journal of Political Economy*, Vol. LXVII (Dec. 1959), pp. 571-579.

6. With James Buchanan (Ann Arbor: University of Michigan Press, 1962).

7. The figures are reproduced in my *Economics of Income Redistribution* (Boston: Kluwer Academic Publishers, 1983), p. 94.

8. Stanley Lebergott, *The American Economy* (Princeton, NJ: Princeton University Press, 1976), p. 57.

9. Professor Dales' tradeable pollution rights on the whole have less susceptibility to rent-seeking activity than pollution taxes.

10. Currently, a variant of this is in use in the Senate. Proposals for additional expenditure must be accompanied either by a proposed tax or a proposed expenditure cut somewhere else.

10 CONCLUDING THOUGHTS

In the fifties, I worked as a specialist on China for the Department of State. I lived in Nationalist and Communist China and in President Rhee's Korea.[1] Although at the time I did not think about rent seeking (indeed, I would have simply called these regimes corrupt),[2] undoubtedly this experience had a lot to do with my eventual discovery of rent seeking.

Particularly in China but also in Korea, I saw ancient high cultures: societies of hard-working, intelligent people who had been civilized for a long time and had produced works of art that were astonishing. These cultures had also had governments that were much admired by travelers up to about 1750, and that had maintained foreign and domestic peace as well as or better than the European governments. In spite of these facts, their citizens were bitterly poor.

There was another aspect of the matter. When I first went to China, I lived in Tientsin in what formerly had been the British concession. By the time I arrived after the Second World War, the concessionary regime had been totally ended, and special privileges for foreigners and for Chinese living inside the foreign concessions had disappeared. It was still true, however, that one could easily tell when one was in a foreign concession, at the border of the foreign concessions the buildings suddenly shrank.³

Another intriguing characteristic was that the foreigners' Tientsin Club was actually outside the foreign concessions, as were a number of foreign homes. Chinese, Russians, and Germans lived inside the concession; wealthy Englishmen and Americans sometimes lived outside before World War II. The reason was simple: Englishmen and Americans carried their extraterritorial privileges with them; Chinese, Russians, and Germans did not. One continuously heard of wealthy Chinese who had a rule of never setting foot outside the concession area.

As a final item, the Tientsin foreign concessions had been put on some swampy land outside what was then the Chinese city of Tientsin. It rapidly became the principal commercial center and had larger buildings and a denser (although smaller) population than the traditional city.

The normal explanation given for this setup by foreigners was that one was out from under control of Chinese government in these areas. There was no obvious superficial reason, however, why one would think that would be an advantage. It is true that at the time I was there the civil war was going on full blast, as it had been from 1911. But in that complex civil war, fighting inside cities, or even shelling or bombing them, was rare. Why, then, were the Chinese fleeing their own government and setting up under what was a set of inferior copies of European governments?

At the time, to repeat, I thought this was corruption. I would now say it was rent seeking. It should be emphasized here that I had been given a pretty thorough introduction into anthropology before I went to the Far East, and I did not put any particular strong negative moral connotation to the word "corruption." I was aware of the fact that the things we refer to as corruption had been going on in China for a long time and were not particularly objected to by the Chinese. Nevertheless, that they would be inefficient seemed obvious.

My feeling that these circumstances were normal was reinforced when the Chinese Communists took over the city. In some ways, this is a throwback to earlier Imperial government, and corruption changed its form, although I do not think it became less common. Last, I spent some time in President Rhee's Korea where I saw more of the same.

I came to the conclusion, then, that the basic reason that the Chinese and, for that matter, the Koreans were so poor, in spite of their high personal qualities and their glorious history, was that this system made economic progress difficult. At the time, I would have been a little hard-pressed to explain why, but now I think the rent-seeking argument explains it.

It is interesting that Ann Krueger, another pioneer in the rent-seeking field (she independently reinvented it), also had extensive experience with non-European cultures, albeit, in her case, India and Turkey were more significant than China. India, in particular, presents much the same problem as China: an obviously high culture, with immense achievements in its past and a bitterly poor population. Jagdish Bhagwati, a third pioneer in rent seeking who is trying to get it called DUP, is actually an Indian, albeit extremely upper class.

All of this puzzled me at the time because Chicago, although corrupt, was nowhere near as badly off. Of course, Chicago was embedded in a society that, for the most part, was not corrupt, which undoubtedly helped. It was also notable that there were a certain number of Chinese in Tientsin (mainly people who had spent most of their lives in the concessions) who were wealthy but lacking in the way of government privileges. They were mainly involved in foreign trade, which lifted them out somewhat from the corrupt society around them.

But to repeat, the word "corrupt" carries with it moral notions that should not be implied here. People were not doing anything regarded as remarkable or susceptible to criticism. The average Chinese was more likely to be offended by the wealthy man who had made his fortune selling rugs in the United States than by the equally well-off mayor of Tientsin.[4] It was thought natural that high political office or friendship with high political figures would lead to a good standard of living. Making money from commerce was thought of as disgraceful.[5]

What I observed, then, was a society in which there were diligent people interested in improving their well-being, but with the idea of doing it by developing personal connections with people of power. As an American vice consul, I found this to some extent a nuisance because I simply could not convince these people that in dealing with the American government, personal connections (particularly with me) were of little help.

I had nothing to do with visas myself, but I was hand carrying visa applications from my desk down to the visa office because the applicant or a friend of a friend of a friend knew me and knew no one in the visa office. On a number of occasions, Chinese who were attempting to get scholarships in American universities asked me if I would pass the application on. My efforts were unsuccessful in convincing them that the admissions officer could hardly care whether he got a letter from an

American vice consul of whom he had never heard. Incidentally, my superiors (whom I feel did not quite understand the local situation) always prohibited me from complying with these requests. I thought it would be harmless and might relieve the nervous tension of the Chinese.

It is notable that these same Chinese, when they get out from under the Chinese government — for example, in the foreign concessions, Hong Kong, or scattered throughout Southeast Asia during the days of the empires there and now in the United States — do very well. In a way, their great interest in both scholarship and personal connections are helpful in Western-type societies. They also recognize that in Western-type societies they cannot depend solely on connections and that they have to "produce" to get ahead. And being people with great talent, they do so.

But the result of this system is that much energy is put into what we now call rent seeking. This has a second effect which I think is at least equally deleterious to economic development. The special privileges that can be obtained are not secure. Another rent seeker may replace you in governmental favor tomorrow. Further, the system treats property as if it were a special privilege. Thus, it is not possible for a person to simply move outside the system and engage in what we in the West call business activities because they are always dominated by this vast rent-seeking apparatus.

Consequently, almost all the talent and energy of the Chinese who wanted to rise in society tended to be directed at efforts to obtain the favor of the powers that be or to retain that favor if they already had it. The life was an insecure one but paid off well for the winners. It also had the characteristic that physical progress was slow. Resources went into things that did not actually produce a consumer surplus for other people, and in most cases, there was a negative externality. If I got appointed as customs inspector, it meant that someone else did not.

My only prior experience with anything like this was in Chicago, and my knowledge of Chicago politics was not great. Further, Chicago, as I have said, was embedded in a larger system that subdued the effect of this type of situation. I now realize that if I had looked around carefully I would have seen signs of it in Chicago or, for that matter, in any American city. The zoning system had been adopted by most American cities in the First World War. It put the owners of large amounts of real estate in a similar situation. The value of many plots depended heavily on more or less arbitrary decisions by officials of the zoning board.

Even if the zoning board were completely clean in the sense that no

CONCLUDING THOUGHTS

outside influence occurred and it made the best possible decisions based on a thorough knowledge of locational economics,[6] the individual would have suffered essentially arbitrary decisions. What he could do on his land would depend not on his well-being but on the well-being of a number of neighbors. The externalities of his decision would be taken into account in a way which, from his standpoint, would almost certainly appear arbitrary. Further, it was certainly true that the real estate industry rapidly developed specialists in manipulating the zoning boards. It also developed corrupt zoning boards.

Although this system is similar to that in places like India today, it does not have the massive negative effect that one would expect simply because, again, it is buried in a system that functions in different ways. All zoning boards are local, and although they make sharp changes in the wealth of the real estate owners, the average citizen who does not own a piece of real estate may not even notice what is going on. A shopping center built on one particular corner and not another does not interest anyone except the owners of those two corners and the people who live fairly close to them. If a whole society worked this way, however, the costs could be, and in backward countries are, immense.

Thus, I am convinced that rent seeking is costly activity when it becomes widespread. In the nineteenth century, we had some in the United States and England, but it was not a far-reaching phenomenon. Further, most countries began copying the essentially English system in the later part of the nineteenth century, with the result that rent seeking shrank in most of the world. It should be emphasized that the reason it shrank was not that we had discovered a magical way of keeping it down, but simply that the total size of government was relatively small.

The organization of private monopoly raises exactly the same problem, but as a matter of fact, it is very difficult to organize private monopolies in a free trade regime. Most of the monopolies that were in any sense extortionate depended on governmental protection.[7]

Direct transfers from and to large parts of the population, such as the Social Security system, raise somewhat different problems. Since Prince Bismarck invented the welfare state, these systems have been a growing part of modern economies. The amounts of money involved in such arrangements are truthfully gigantic, although strictly speaking, the transfer component is not all that big. Medical insurance schemes, for example, are sometimes private and sometimes governmental. If we cashed out the government programs by purchasing private insurance policies for everyone and compared this with such programs as the

English national health system, we would notice that the national scheme was somewhat more egalitarian than the private insurance, but not much.[8]

The same is true of old age pensions once they have been established. They are basically inefficient in the sense that if the system is left unchanged over your lifetime, you would have done better by saving and investing your insurance premiums. These systems are to some extent progressive in that they transfer funds to the lower middle class by taking the money from the poor and from the upper classes, but again, the transfer is rather small.[9]

The problem here is that in most Western societies it is rather hard to put your finger on the direct cost of these large programs. For most people, the effect of the program as opposed to buying insurance is rather small.[10] Further, calculating the actual effect is difficult. Thus, the rent-seeking effort may be small compared to the apparent size of the transfer. As I dictate this, I am reading an advance copy of a book, *One Billion Dollars of Influence: The Direct Marketing of Politics*.[11] It deals only with one aspect of the government influence of business: specifically, direct mail advertising. A billion dollars seems small, given the amounts of money at risk.

The same is true if one looks at the people who take congressmen to expensive restaurants, and so on, in Washington. It is a big number, absolutely, but considering what is at stake, it appears to be small.

I remain convinced that all of this is simply the foam on the real concealed cost. In particular, the type of concealment I talk about in the second and third chapters of this book is important.[12] Both of these phenomena are obviously large, but it is hard to measure either one.

In summary, in my opinion rent seeking is an extremely costly phenomenon that severely damages our society. Measuring that cost, or even putting one's finger on it, is difficult. The first section of this book has been devoted to pointing out the problems in measuring, and pointing out ways in which they might be overcome. The second section is more diverse. If rent seeking is as important as I think, then it is sensible to work on the theory.

In this section, I discuss a number of areas where I believe the theory needs improvement. The individual articles are not closely connected except that they are all relevant to rent seeking. The two previous books on rent seeking[13] are both collections of essays, some of which had been published previously. In a way, the second section of this book is a continuation of those two earlier books, while the first section, in essence, is one long essay on a particular topic.

I would like to close this chapter and the book the same way I began part II: by a discussion of the proper definition of rent seeking. As I have said earlier, my definitions of the term are relatively crude. We need a general definition permitting us to take into account the waste both of inappropriate economic institutions and of what we might call overinvestment in sales effort. Unfortunately, we do not have it. We have no way of measuring the overinvestment in sales effort in cases where the ultimate outcome is itself desirable.

My solution to this problem is simply to confine the term rent seeking to institutions like protective tariffs that we know are inefficient. Thus, we discuss the costs of getting a protective tariff through, in terms of rent seeking and use "rent avoidance" for the cost of fighting against a protective tariff. The cost of selling soap is not included in either term. To repeat, I would like to have a continuous function that takes all three things into account, but, for the time being, I think we are stuck with the somewhat more limited application of rent seeking.

Regardless of whether the reader agrees with my definition, I hope it will at least be given careful thought. Indeed, that is my hope with respect to this whole book. Rent seeking is a new field, one in which there is far more work to be done. This book is, to quote Chairman Mao Tse-tung, merely the "first step in the ten thousand li march."

Notes

1. I had also lived, while in college and while briefly practicing law, in the Chicago of the Kelly-Nash regime. In some ways, this rather resembled President Rhee's Korea.
2. Also Chicago.
3. Incidentally, the same is true of Monaco. On the streets that make up the boundaries of that principality, average height of the buildings on either side of the street differs.
4. Either the Nationalist or the Communist mayor. The Communist mayor, as a matter of fact, lived better than the Nationalist mayor, but this reflected the fact that the Nationalist mayor was, by the not very stringent standards of the Nationalist government, a rather Spartan type.
5. Under the Imperial regime, merchants and, in particular, bankers were among the group called outcasts listed with actors, prostitutes, and so on. Some wealthy merchants connected with foreign trade in Hong Kong and Macao were, however, able to get around these barriers.
6. I do not think any location economist believes he/she can make perfect decisions of this sort, but he/she can do better than the average politician.
7. There apparently were some cases in the early days of modern industry in which some particular company actually had enough advantage in efficiency so that it effectively obtained a monopoly by underselling everyone else. But if this happened occasionally, in spite of the Austrians, we should not depend on it.

8. The basic criticisms of governmental health service are mainly concerned with the efficiency with which it operates, not with its rather modest egalitarianism. To paraphrase Milton Friedman: it is a requirement that everyone buy a particular insurance contract, and not a very good one.

9. The transfer from the poor comes from the fact that the truthfully poor would have, in fact, been receiving state aid even if the old age pension system did not exist. The same, incidentally, it true of the government medical insurance. Thus the poor are relatively no better off in their medical treatment and their old age pension than they would be if these programs had not have been created and they had depended on the more traditional forms of aid to the poor. On the other hand, their taxes are considerably higher than they would have been under the anci'en regime. All of this is discussed in detail in my *Economics of Income Redistribution* (Boston: Kluwer-Nijhoff, 1983), 111-136.

10. Given the fact that there is risk attached to both governmental and private insurance, risk aversion would point to splitting insurance between them.

11. R. Kenneth Godwin (Chatham, NJ: Chatham House Publishers House, Inc., 1988). The billion dollars is a measure of the whole industry, not its effect on a given election or proposed bill.

12. The third chapter deals with the metaphysical problem of whether it is actually a cost. Subjectively, I think it is a cost. Certainly the growth of the economy would be slower with this kind of thing than without it.

13. *Towards a Theory of the Rent-Seeking Society*, James M. Buchanan, Robert D. Tollison, and Gordon Tullock (eds.)(College Station: Texas A&M University Press, 1981) and *The Political Economy of Rent-Seeking*, Charles K. Rowley, Robert D. Tollison, and Gordon Tullock (eds.)(Boston: Kluwer Academic Publishers, 1988).

BIBLIOGRAPHY

Becker, Gary. "Public Policies, Pressure Groups, and Dead Weight Costs." *Journal of Public Economics* 28, 1985, pp. 329–347.

Brennan, Geoffrey and James Buchanan. "Voter Choice: Evaluating Political Alternatives." *American Behavioral Scientists* 29, November/December 1984, pp. 185–201.

Buchanan, James and Gordon Tullock. *The Calculus of Consent.* Ann Arbor: University of Michigan Press, 1962.

Derthick, Martha and Paul J. Quirk. *The Politics of Deregulation.* Washington D.C.: Brookings, 1985.

Downs, Anthony. *An Economics Analysis of Democracy.* New York: Harper, 1957.

Godwin, R. Kenneth. *One Billion Dollars of Influence: The Direct Marketing of Politics.* Chatham, NJ: Chatham House, 1989.

Harsanyi, J. C. "Games with Randomly Distributed Payoffs: A New Rationale for Mixed Strategy Equilibrium Points." *International Journal of Game Theory* 2, 1973, pp. 1–23.

Hillman, Arye L. and D. Samet. "Dissipation of Rents by a Small Number of Contenders." *Public Choice* 54, No. 1, 1987, pp. 63–82.

Lebergott, Stanley. *The American Economy.* Princeton, NJ: Princeton University Press, 1976.

Libecap, Gary D. "Political Economy of Fuel Oil Cartelization by the Texas Railroad Commission 1933–1972." August 1977. Unpublished.

Miller, James C. III. "Policy Making in Washington: Some Personal Observations." *Southern Economic Journal*, 1984, p. 395.

Muller, Dennis. *Public Choice II*. New Rochelle, NY: Cambridge University Press. Forthcoming.

Olson, Mancur. *The Logic of Collective Action: Public Goods and the Theory of Groups*. Cambridge, MA: Harvard University Press, 1965.

Peltzman, Samuel. "Toward a More General Theory of Regulation." *Journal of Law and Economics*, August 1976.

Reich, Robert B. and John D. Donahue. *New Deals, The Chrysler Revival and the American System*. New York: Penguin Books, 1986. Pp. 204–205.

Schumpeter, Joseph A. *Capitalism, Socialism and Democracy*. New York: Harper and Bros., 1942.

Stein, Herbert. "Balancing the Budget) Compared with What?" *AEI Economist*, February 1987.

The Political Economy of Rent-Seeking. Charles K. Rowley, Robert D. Tollison, and Gordon Tullock, eds. Boston: Kluwer Academic Publishers, 1988.

Tollison, Robert D. and Gary Anderson. "Luddism as Cartel Support." *Journal of Institutional and Theoretical Economics*, December 1986, pp. 727–738.

Tucson Citizen, 11 March 1988, p. A-1.

Tullock, Gordon. "Problems of Majority Voting." *Journal of Political Economy* 67, December 1959, pp. 571–579.

———"Information Without Profit." *Papers on Non-Market Decision Making* Vol. I. Charlottesville, VA: Thomas Jefferson Center for Political Economy, 1966, pp. 141–159.

———*The Organization of Inquiry*. Durham: Duke University Press, 1966; and New York: University Press of America, 1987.

———"The Welfare Costs of Monopolies, Tariffs, and Theft." *Western Economic Journal* 5, Fall 1967, pp. 224–232; rpt. *Towards a Theory of the Rent-Seeking Society*. James M. Buchanan, Robert D. Tollison and Gordon Tullock, eds. College Station: Texas A&M University Press, 1980. Pp. 39-50.

———"Simple Algebraic Logrolling." *American Economic Review* 60, June 1970, pp. 419–426.

———"Charity of the Uncharitable." *Western Economic Journal* 9, December 1971, pp. 379–392.

———"The Cost of Transfers." *Kyklos* 24, December 1971, pp. 629–643.

———*Towards a Mathematics of Politics*. Ann Arbor: University of Michigan Press, 1976.

———"Regulating the Regulators." *Government Controls and the Free Market: The U.S. Economy in the 1970s*. Svetozar Pejovich, ed. College Station: Texas A&M University Press, 1976. Pp. 141–159.

———"Efficient Rent Seeking." *Toward a Theory of the Rent-Seeking Society*. James

M. Buchanan, Robert D. Tollison, and Gordon Tullock, eds. College Station: Texas A&M University Press, 1980. Pp. 97–112.

———*Economics of Income Redistribution*. Boston: Kluwer-Nijhoff, 1983.

———"Back to the Bog." *Public Choice* 46, No. 3, 1985, pp. 259–263; rpt. *The Political Economy of Rent-Seeking*. Charles K. Rowley, Robert D. Tollison, and Gordon Tullock, eds. Boston: Kluwer Academic Publishers, 1988. Pp. 141–146.

———"Intellectual Property." *Direct Protection of Innovation*, William Kingston, ed. Dordrecht: Kluwer Academic Press, 1987. Pp. 171–199.

———"Another Part of the Swamp." *Public Choice* 54, No. 1, 1987, pp. 83–84.

———"The Costs of Rent-Seeking: A Metaphysical Problem." *Public Choice* 57, April 1988, pp. 15–24.

———"Rents and Rent Seeking." *The Political Economy of Rent-Seeking*. Charles K. Rowley, Robert D. Tollison, and Gordon Tullock, eds. Boston: Kluwer Academic Publishers, 1988. Pp. 51–62.

Harsanyi, John, 70
Hillman, A. L., 69–70

Income tax, 80–81
Insurance, 95–96
Interstate Commerce Commission (ICC), 24

Japanese automobile industry, 22–23

Korea, 91, 92–93
Krueger, Ann, 93

Libecap, Gary D., 12

Markets, 59–66
Medical insurance, 95–96
Monopolies, 20, 95
Moral principles, 6–7, 21–22

Nash equilibrium, 67, 69, 71

Olson, Mancur, 43

Patents, 49–50, 53–54
Peltzman, Samuel, 13, 22
Pensions, 96
Politicians
  balancing in interchanges with, 22–23
  tax loopholes and, 82–84
  voters and rent-seeking activities of, 5–6, 37
Production, inefficient methods in, 13–17
Profits, 62–63
Public image of rent seekers, 19–21
Public interest, 31–32

Quirk, Paul J., 24
Quotas, in automobile industry, 22–23, 84

Real estate, 94–95
Rent seeking
  costs of, 5, 29–38, 96
  definition problem in, 49–56
  inefficiency in production and, 13–17
  inefficiency in transfer of, 12–13, 18–19, 23
  loss in, 15
  markets and, 59–66
  mathematical problem of efficiency in, 6
  morality and, 6–7
  observational problems in, 11–12
  social waste and, 24–25
  tax reform and, 79–88
  transfers and, 73–77
Rent-seeking industry
  diseconomy of scale in, 41–44, 63–66
  possible explanations for inefficiency of, 5–7
  public image of, 19–21
  size of, 1–45
Research, and patents, 49–50, 53–54

Samet, D., 69–70
Schumpeter, Joseph A., 32
Stein, Herbert, 30

Taft, William Howard, 33
Tax reform, 79–88
Texas Railroad Commission, 12
Transfers, 73–77
Tucson Air Pollution Reduction Program, 18–19

United Auto Workers (UAW), 23

Voters
  costs of rent seeking and, 29–30
  government programs and, 21
  moral principles of, 21–22
  rent-seeking activities of politicians and, 5–6, 37

Zoning system, 94–95

INDEX

Advertising, 51–53
Agricultural programs, 15–16, 19
Airline industry, 13, 20
Air pollution, 82, 86
Automobile industry, 22–23, 84–85

Becker, Gary S., 13, 22
Bentham, Jeremy, 34
Bhagwati, Jagdish, 93
Bryan, William Jennings, 33
Buchanan, James, 87

Campaign contributions, 12
China, 91–95
Civil Aeronautics Board (CAB), 13, 20, 24
Competition, 54–55
Consumer Products Safety Commission, 3, 4
Costs of rent seeking, 5, 29–38, 96
　choices made by individuals and, 29–30
　externalities and, 34–35
　information and, 35–36

　public interest and, 31–32
　special interests and, 32–33
　transfers and, 74–75, 77

Depletion allowance, 81
Derthick, Martha, 24
Diseconomies of scale, 41–44
Downs, Anthony, 21

Economies of scale, 41–44, 63–66
Environmental Protection Administration, 82

Farm lobby, 19

Government
　agricultural programs of, 15–16, 19
　competition and, 54–55
　restriction programs of, 16